Contemporary Quilting

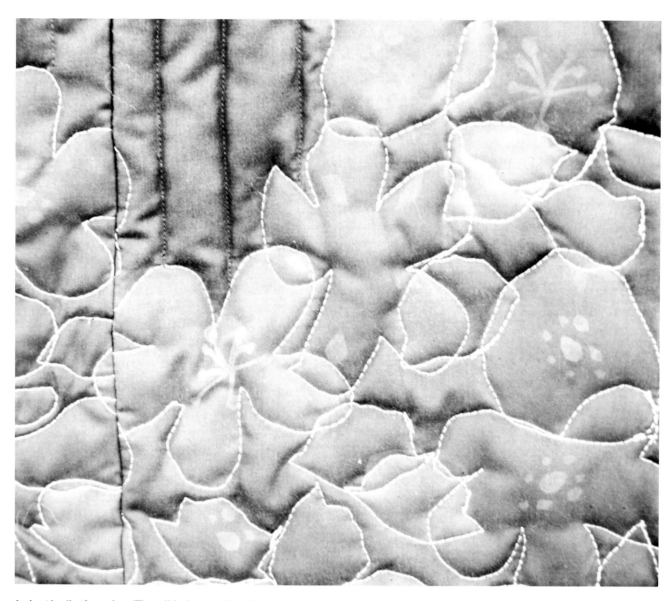

Jacket (detail), the author. The polished cotton fabric has been air-brushed with a floral pattern and then quilted with silver metallic threads.

Sharon Robinson

CONTEMPORARY QUILTING

Davis Publications, Inc.

Worcester, Massachusetts

Also by Sharon Robinson
Contemporary Basketry

Printed in the United States of America
Library of Congress Catalog Card Number: 81-66572
ISBN: 0-87192-134-0

Graphic Design: Jane Pitts

10 9 8 7 6 5 4 3 2 1

Contents

Dedicated in memory of my Grandma

Stella Reddingius Robinson.

She, too, liked to make quilts.

Crib Quilt, **Stella Reddingius Robinson. 34″ × 42″. This
blue and white quilt was hand embroidered for the author
by her grandmother.**

Acknowledgments

I would like to thank all the artists who have allowed
me to use their work in this book. It was a pleasure
and a great deal of fun writing to you.

Thanks to my friend Carolyn Finley for answering
many questions. And thanks again to my daughter,
Cathie, who demonstrated many of the quilting techniques pictured in the book.

Contemporary Quilting

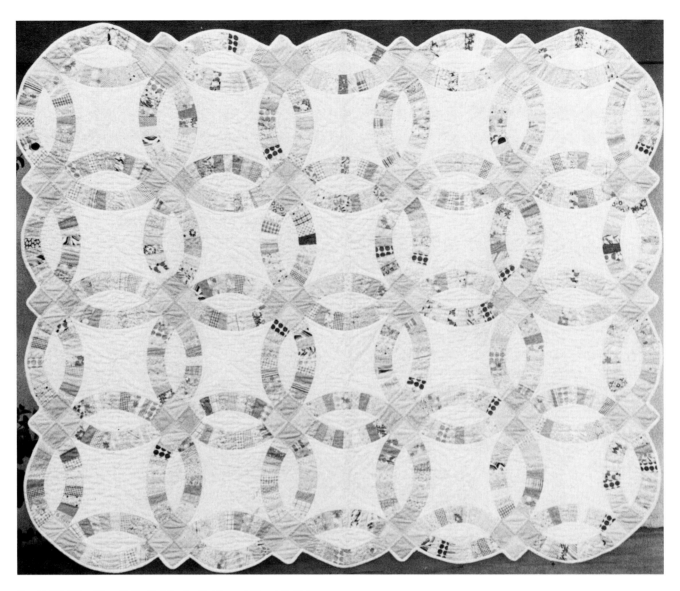

Double Wedding Ring, Stella Reddingius Robinson. 72″ × 90″. This quilt is multicolored on a white background. Courtesy of Pat and Joe Moody.

Chapter One

INTRODUCTION

As textiles do not survive well, we will never know exactly when or where the first quilted pieces were made. Evidence does show that the ancient Chinese and Egyptians used quilting techniques on their clothing. Undoubtedly, this craft had numerous beginnings as people around the world have had the need to keep warm.

Europeans probably first saw quilting in the eleventh and twelfth centuries when the Crusaders returned home with some quilted textiles. Early colonists to the New World, in turn, brought quilting skills and designs to this country. During the American Colonial period, quilting went in a new direction as piecing designs began to develop. This quilting technique replaced the European one of having a single overall design on one large cloth. Instead, the colonists created a block only a few inches square which could be repeated. The blocks were sewn together later to create an overall pattern. This technique very likely developed for practical reasons such as lack of work space and the necessity of using fabric scraps.

Quilting continued to spread as people moved West and took their needle arts with them. Quilting bees became important social events for both working and visiting. Notes on quilt patterns were compared. Quilting continued to grow and develop until industrialization ended the need for this domestic art. Fortunately, Southern mountaineers (and a few determined individuals) kept many crafts, such as quilting, alive during this period.

Colonial women brought a new spirit and growth to the quilting of their European sisters. Today there is another rebirth of this art. In the 1960s quiltmaking and other crafts began to be accepted as contemporary art forms. In the past, quilting was chiefly valued for its utilitarian function of covering a bed or keeping a body warm. Once "necessity" was removed, the craft was free to be fully created as an art, to be appreciated for itself alone. As the craft today still contains the element of usefulness, it is all the more intriguing. Contemporary artists may draw upon the craft's history when creating new forms.

As you look at old quilts sometimes you will find one that contains a very personal and indeed artistic statement. This is the quilt that has more to say than "good craftsmanship," "good design" and "old fabric scraps." One can't help but wonder if the quiltmaker felt frustrated and lonely for someone to appreciate her artistic statement. She must have known that quiltmaking was more than a domestic chore. I wish she could see the quilts that are being constructed today.

While today's quilts are influenced by historical forms, they display many new features. Quilts are made using new and unusual fabrics as well as old. Quiltmakers, no longer dependent upon remnants from earlier sewing projects, may choose cloth that is ideal for personal expression. They may even dye fabrics themselves to achieve a value or hue not found in stores. New kinds of synthetic batting, threads, and other notion materials are available to today's artist that did not exist in the past.

The form of the quilt is changing also. Quiltmakers, who are now men as well as women, are not feeling the restrictions of a square or a rectangle, but are creating in a wide variety of shapes and sizes. Quilts are hung on walls and sometimes draped to form reliefs. They lie on floors or tables. Or they become sculptures. Form in quilting is exciting today. All of these features and more contribute to today's contemporary quilt.

This book explains and illustrates techniques. It contains an excellent collection of contemporary work using quilting, piecing, and appliqué as the art form. In preparation for your own creations, experiment with various techniques and materials while using this book. Each has its own characteristics and through experimentation you will find what pleases you. Also, begin to look around you for sources of inspiration. Study quilt shows, books, and most especially, your surroundings. You will find that the most inspired art comes from people who are able to see and understand their environment.

Chapter Two

MATERIALS AND TOOLS

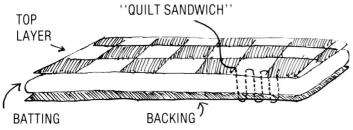

TOP LAYER

"QUILT SANDWICH"

BATTING

BACKING

In this book, "quilt" refers to any quilted piece, not just a bed quilt. A quilt is usually composed of three layers—the top, the filling, and the backing—and the threads or yarn that join them.

Basically, there are two processes involved in making a quilt. The first is the designing and making of the quilt's surface, or top layer. This may be done by appliqué or piecing. The second step is quilting the top together with a backing and filling material to produce the finished quilt.

Selecting and combining materials for this "quilt sandwich" is a challenging process requiring forethought and experimentation. This chapter provides an overview of important considerations, materials, and tools for quilting projects. Items discussed in relation to specific techniques are described more fully in later chapters.

Materials

Fabrics

Selecting from today's exciting and varied fabrics can be complicated. You must be able to identify a fabric to know how it can perform and be used in the best way. These steps cannot be overemphasized for working successfully with fabrics.

Identifying a fabric can be confusing. We not only have the natural fibers of wool, linen, cotton, rayon, and silk, but technology also has created a multitude of synthetic fabrics. One can be confused by the great number of generic fiber names as well as trade names used. A good fabric handbook helps provide clear information, see Bibliography.

Identifying a fiber will enable you to understand its characteristics and predict how it will perform. Some important considerations are: Will it wrinkle? Can it be washed? What ironing temperature should be used? Sometimes one fiber may have the characteristics of another. For instance, wrinkle-free is a highly desirable attribute for a fabric. Polyester has this quality. Because cotton wrinkles, it often undergoes a wrinkle-free treatment. It is wise to know all about a fabric before purchasing it, and it is important to learn what is the best fabric for your purposes.

Before selecting fabric, completely work out plans for your quilted project. You may wish to make changes as you proceed, but it helps to start with a good plan. Plan not only the design, but how the piece will be used. Will your quilt provide warmth or will it be a wall hanging? Will it need frequent washing or an occasional vacuuming? Care is important. You may need a wrinkle-free fabric, as finished quilts should not be ironed. Unlike utilitarian textiles, an art work need not be washable. For example, fabrics may be chosen for a wall hanging simply because of their texture or sheen and not their cleaning characteristics. For a bed quilt or a jacket, however, the cleaning method is important. Fabrics that wash or dry clean are then a must. When using a variety of fabrics in a garment, choose types that may be cleaned in the same manner.

For the beginner, 100 percent cotton is the best. It is a durable fabric, will not ravel, may be ripped, has good body, will not stretch out of shape, and is easy to handle. Calico, a plain woven fabric with a small, contrasting print design, is popular. Cottons also should be opaque unless transparency is desirable for some special effect.

Be sure the fabric has an "even weave"—that is, there are as many threads per inch in the warp as in the weft. Warp refers to the threads which run lengthwise—the strongest direction of the fabric. Weft describes the threads which run across the fabric. The threads of your fabric should be smooth—not nubby. A wrinkle-free treatment on the surface may be desirable. A finished quilted surface cannot be ironed because the filling will be flattened, but some 100 percent cottons smooth out very well after washing.

Avoid cotton and polyester blends because most of them ravel. Always preshrink washable fabrics—even those that supposedly will not shrink—to avoid problems later. If a fabric is stretched out of shape, it must be stretched back into place to prepare it for cutting on the grain, the length of the fabric.

The more creative you become with your quilts, the more you will use a variety of fabrics. You will want characteristics in your fabric that cotton cannot provide. Before choosing new materials, however, understand their characteristics and your needs.

Batting

Batting is the soft material in the center of the quilt sandwich. You may buy it by the yard or bed size. Choose type and thickness according to the requirements of the piece. If you want warmth, a thick batt may be best. However, it is more difficult to handle on the machine than a thinner one.

Many years ago, batts were made by putting together layers of carded wool or cotton. Today, most are made of polyester fiber. Some batts are "bonded" to make them more manageable. Bonding makes them firmer so they will not fall apart when used or washed. Some batts are bonded on the surface only, while others are bonded all the way through. Both types are good to use. Another type of polyester batt has a surface that is laminated with a thin layer of polyester foam. This prevents the fibers from working their way up through the top or backing.

Cotton batts are available but will tend to "lump up" when used. They require more stitches per square inch than a polyester batt when assembling the "quilt sandwich." Again, keep your purpose in mind when selecting the fiber content and characteristics of the batt.

Backing Fabric

The fabric used for the bottom layer of the quilt sandwich should be chosen according to your needs. If the backing is an integral part of the quilt, then the fabrics and color will require careful consideration. If the backing fabric will not show, a less expensive (but not inferior) fabric may be used. Also to be considered is the weight of the backing fabric. The backing should not be heavier than the top of the quilt as it may cause awkward pulling or stretching out of shape. A fabric equal or lighter in weight to that of the top is the best choice.

Threads

Another consideration is how the layers of your quilted piece will be sewn together. Will it be tied or quilted; machine or hand sewn? What type of thread should be used? By deciding what the needs of the quilt are, you may choose techniques and materials accordingly. Is it utilitarian or non-functional? Do you wish to make the surface elegant or plain? Answers to such questions will narrow the choices.

Traditional quilters feel that hand quilting is the only way to put a quilt together. Contemporary quilters choose the sewing technique to complement the total design of the quilt. Machine sewing is much faster than hand sewing. However, batting and much yardage make it bulky to handle and you may not save as much time with a machine as you expected. Sometimes there is a technical reason for choosing the machine over the hand method of quilting. For instance, if you wish to use a metallic thread to quilt a surface, you will need a machine. A large needle on your sewing machine will open a space large enough for the metallic thread to slide through without falling apart. Small hand sewn stitches using metallics would not be possible as the thread would fall apart. Further aesthetic and technical considerations will be discussed in chapter 5.

Several types of thread are available for sewing pieces together and for quilting. Traditional quilters use only 100 percent cotton thread in their hand sewing and quilting. It is easy to use and does not twist as it is being worked by hand through the fabric. However, some brands of cotton covered polyester threads work very well on the machine and may be treated with beeswax (available in small chunks in fabric stores) for hand sewing. To apply it, simply run the thread between your thumb and the chunk. In addition, there are threads to create a special effect, like metallics and heavy threads.

Tools

Tools are vital to carrying out your quilting ideas. Most are readily available at notion counters while others, like drafting triangles and T squares, can be found in art supply stores. Check the notion counters for tools such as sewing machine accessories and markers. Stationery and hardware stores, art and craft suppliers, fabric and yarn shops should have all the tools you need.

Scissors

For cutting fabric, use only sharp dressmaker shears. Never use these scissors on paper since this will quickly dull the edge. You can cut threads quickly and easily with thread snips.

Marking Tools

Direct Markers. There are several tools for marking a design or guidelines on fabric, and they should be chosen carefully. Ball-point pens mark fabric rapidly and are especially good for use with a yardstick. However, their ink is permanent and must be used carefully to avoid damage to the cloth. Felt markers are good for preparing fabric for cutting. A water soluble felt marker is not recommended since it will bleed and cause a stain when the fabric is washed.

Disappearing pens are nicknamed "spit pens" because their marks come off when moistened. First, check to see if it will come off your particular type of fabric when moistened. Also, check that the pen is not made permanent by detergent or by setting with the iron.

Pictured here are spools of cotton quilting thread, cotton covered polyester thread, and large spools of metallic and heavy denim sewing thread.

According to your needs, you may select from a variety of pencils, pens, and chalks to mark fabric directly.

Pictured is a roll of transfer paper (which also comes in sheets), dressmaker tracing paper with wheel, and a pad of tracing paper.

Tailor chalk is also very good for drawing on fabric directly and will rub off when necessary. However, it may not be the best choice for marking large pieces as it may rub off before work is complete. Another handy marker is a soap sliver. When your bars of soap become too thin for washing hands, use them to mark fabrics. They make a nice thin line.

This design was drawn on a yoke pattern with a heat transfer pencil. To be transferred to the fabric it will be placed face down, pinned in place, and then transferred by the heat of an iron.

Graphite pencil marks are washable. Any type may be used on fabric. A hard pencil will give a lighter and thinner line and will not require sharpening as often as a softer pencil. A soft pencil will make a wide, dark line which is not as crisp as a hard pencil's, and it requires frequent sharpening.

Indirect Markers. There are other methods for marking fabric which are indirect and used for transferring a prepared design onto the fabric. Check to make sure these methods of marking can be removed by washing and pressing a marked sample cloth.

One method is dressmaker carbon and a tracing wheel. This is a carbon paper for fabric which is applied by using a tracing wheel that perforates the paper and makes a line of tiny dots. A design drawn on paper may be transferred to fabric by putting dressmaker carbon between the drawing and the fabric and applying the tracing wheel. It may be especially useful.

A similar transfer may be made using transfer paper. This paper may be purchased at an art supply store. It is thin paper that has graphite on one side. It is used by slipping a sheet between the drawing and the fabric. You may then apply the pressure of a tracing wheel or a pencil to the drawing to transfer the design.

A heat transfer pencil will transfer a design very accurately. This is similar to the heat transfer patterns that may be purchased, only you draw your own design. Make your design on tracing paper using your heat transfer pencil. Do this by tracing over a previous sketch. Now place the finished tracing face down on the fabric. Pin it in place and apply the heat of the iron. Notice that the transferred design will be reversed. Pads of tracing paper may be purchased in art supply stores. Heat transfer pencils are sold in yarn and fabric stores.

Sewing Machine Attachments

Most sewing machines have guides marked right on the machine to direct the fabric as you sew. When sewing the inner part of the quilt, however, they will not be much help because you can't see them. In such cases, guides may be attached to the machine to allow you to line up the seam being sewn with the seam previously sewn.

Occasionally, a special foot is added to the machine for specific techniques. An appliqué or embroidery foot has a large hole around the needle area to provide good visibility while you sew the satin stitch. A roller foot, unlike a regular presser foot, has three rollers. As a result, it applies less weight to fabrics as it slides over their surface, prevents them from shifting during machine quilting, and also keeps knit fabrics from stretching. When putting in zippers, attach a zipper foot. It may also be used for sewing a fabric that has bulk on only one side of the sewing needle, such as for making piping.

Use a zipper foot to prepare piping for a finish on a quilt.

Needles

The needle chosen must accommodate your thread choice. In some cases, heavy threads may be wrapped on the bobbin for machine sewing. A finer needle will be required when using normal size threads and fabrics. Occasionally, specialty needles are required for the machine. A ball-point needle, for example, is used on knit fabrics to prevent threads from breaking, which causes raveling. Leather needles, unlike ordinary ones, will not stick in leather. You may wish to ask your sewing machine dealer for assistance.

Quilting needles, used for hand quilting, are short and strong. They are called "betweens." Choose a size according to the thickness of the fabrics and batting. For hand sewing pieces of fabric together and doing appliqué, use a needle called a "sharp." A size #8 or #10 is recommended. "Sharps" are long needles and therefore several small stitches may be put on the needle before pulling it through the fabric.

Old Maid's Fancy, Susan Wise. 5′ × 7′. This quilt is a mixture of cotton fabrics, embroidered and appliquéd by hand. The piecing and the quilting were done by machine. Photograph by Ralph Fleming.

(opposite) *God Bless America*, Phyllis Williams. This denim skirt is made of various materials such as: satin, velvet, velveteen, corduroy, velour, jersey, silver thread, embroidery floss, and rhinestones. The techniques are appliqué and embroidery. Photograph by Quicksilver Photography, Columbus, Ohio.

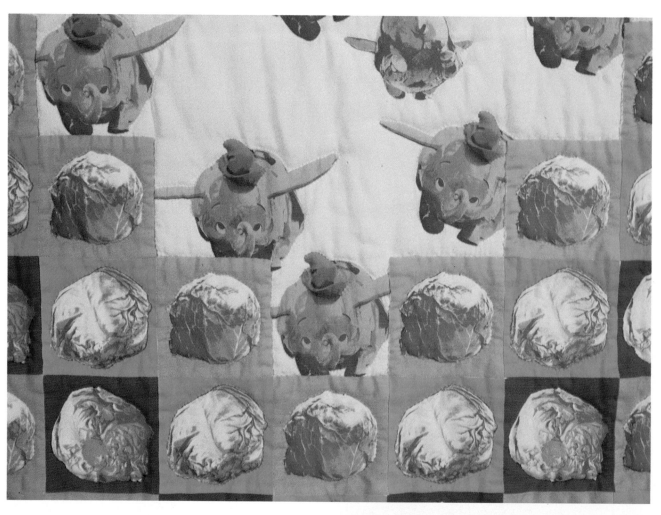

California Cabbage Patchwork, **Detail.**

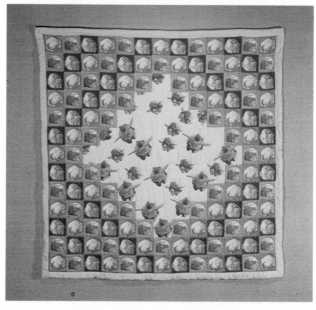

California Cabbage Patchwork, **Marna Goldstein. 66″ × 66″. This photo-silkscreened piece was pieced, appliquéd, and then hand quilted using cotton fabric. Photograph by the artist.**

Kapa Rain of Honolulu, Marie Robertson. 86″ × 86″. This Hawaiian quilt was made from a traditional pattern in red and off-white. The fabrics are cotton and polyester blends. It was made for the Ford Museum in Dearborn, Michigan. Photograph by Helena Skaer.

Sand Dollar and Seaweed, Jean Davidson. 12″ × 12″. Made of 100% cotton, this piece was constructed using appliqué and reverse appliqué techniques. Photograph by the artist.

Chapter Three

APPLIQUÉ

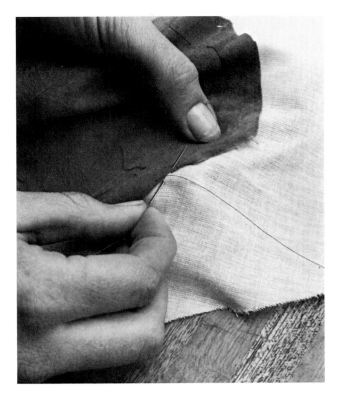

Appliqué is being applied by folding the hem under as the stitching progresses. This appliqué piece was pinned in place because it is small. With larger work, it is advisable to baste the pieces down before beginning to hand stitch.

Direct Appliqué

Appliqué is the application of one piece of fabric on top of another. The applied or top piece is a cut design which may be attached to the background fabric in a variety of ways. The technique may be used alone or with others. Appliqué designs are usually planned but may be drawn directly with pencil on the fabric. Appliqué allows more freedom in design than *pieced* work, the sewing together of small pieces of fabric to create a pattern, as you may draw designs with curved lines. There are a variety of ways to do appliqué.

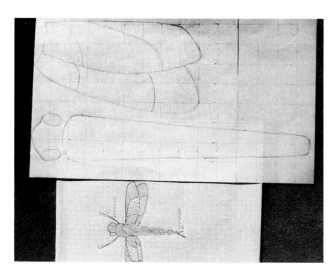

This design was transferred from graph paper (four squares per inch) to paper drawn with a grid of 1″ squares.

A design is being transferred using transfer paper.

Patterns may be traced, but your most rewarding work will come from your own designs. It is a good idea to have the entire design worked out before beginning. A drawing (in small scale) may be made on graph paper to indicate the final arrangement of the design. The individual appliqué pieces to be cut out must be drawn to the correct size. If you need to enlarge a design from graph paper (four squares per inch), transfer your design to a larger piece of paper on which you have drawn a larger grid.

If you are going to repeat an appliqué design several times, you will need to make a template, see chapter 4. Make this template the size of the piece itself, allowing no margin. Now, press your fabric. If you are using a template, place it on the right side of the fabric and draw around it with a pencil. If you are not using a template, transfer the design to the right side of the fabric with dressmaker's carbon or transfer paper. In either case, be sure to leave enough space between designs to allow for a ¼″ margin around each piece. The drawn or transferred line is the seam line. Now, cut the fabric ¼″ beyond it.

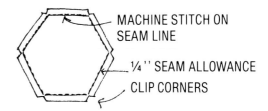

MACHINE STITCH ON SEAM LINE

¼″ SEAM ALLOWANCE

CLIP CORNERS

On the sewing machine, stitch (with a small stitch) on the drawn line. Then, clip the margins on the curves and at the corners, so that they will fold under nicely. Clip close to the stitched line but not into it. After clipping the margins, put the piece in place and pin it down. It may then be basted to the background fabric. The margins will turn under nicely as you blindstitch around the piece. A blindstitch is used when the stitching is to be invisible. The machine stitching line may be used to anchor the hand stitching thread so there will not be fraying around the clipped areas. The machine stitching line will also help to create a nice curve on the curved areas. The ideal appliqué piece is not totally flat, but slightly raised from the foundation fabric. This technique ensures this result.

Another technique is to put the template on the wrong side of the appliqué piece, matching it with the seam lines. With the iron press the margins up and over the template. Remove the template from the piece. The piece is now put where it is needed on the background fabric. Pin and baste into place, then hand stitch.

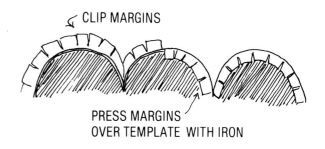

CLIP MARGINS

PRESS MARGINS OVER TEMPLATE WITH IRON

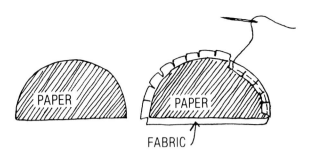

PAPER

PAPER

FABRIC

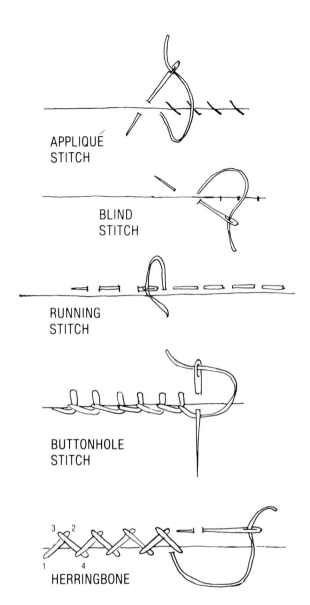

APPLIQUÉ
STITCH

BLIND
STITCH

RUNNING
STITCH

BUTTONHOLE
STITCH

3 2

1   4

HERRINGBONE

Another method of working is to cut the appliqué design out of lightweight paper (allow no margins). Also cut the design out of fabric (include margins). Pin the piece of paper to the wrong side of the fabric piece lining up the edges of the paper to the seam lines. Clip the margins of the fabric on the curves and at the corners. Baste the margins over the paper, see chapter 4. The appliqué piece may then be pinned and hand stitched into place. When completed, the background fabric may be turned over and cut away in the area of the appliqué. Cut up to the ¼″ margins. Cut the basting thread and then the piece of paper may be removed. But while removing the paper may seem to be the logical next step, leaving it in place may be the start of an idea for a very creative quilt. Perhaps the fabric could be sheer so the paper will be seen through it, exposing something of interest. Old quilts were made using newspaper and love-letters—the possibilities are endless.

If using more than one layer of appliqué, cut and place the background pieces first. You may determine where the pieces go by marking the area. This may be done by drawing the entire design on the background fabric or it may be marked by folding the background fabric and lightly pressing it to correspond with the graph paper lines on the original

The first layer of appliqué is sewn permanently in place. The second layer is pinned on top to be first basted and then blindstitched.

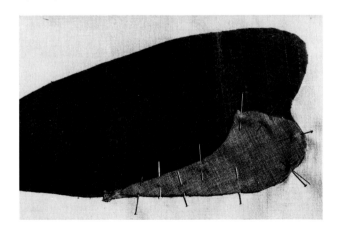

drawing. The pieces are then put in place, see Hawaiian Appliqué.

Appliquéd pieces may be stitched by hand or by machine. How they are to be sewn should be determined before cutting the individual appliquéd pieces. The procedures just described should be followed when hand stitching, either ornamental or hidden, is to be used. When stitching by hand, use a blindstitch with matching thread. Fancy stitches with contrasting thread may be used to attach appliqué pieces. If they are to be stitched on the machine with the zig-zag stitch, pieces do not need to be cut with a margin for turning under, as the machine stitching will cover the raw edges of each piece. Machine zig-zag (or satin) stitching, either in matching or contrasting thread will create an interest of its own.

The rectangle has been appliquéd with fusable interfacing, and the hexagon is being stuffed with a small amount of batting to make it "puff up." They are both satin stitched on the machine.

Whether stitching by machine or by hand, it is possible to create a surface that will "puff up." As you are stitching, stuff a small amount of batting or fiberfill behind the appliqué pieces.

Appliqué pieces may be attached to the background fabric through the use of fusable interfacing. Choose the type that is fusable on both sides to adhere the appliqué piece to the background fabric. Cut it with the template as you did the appliqué piece, allowing no margins for either. Place the interfacing between the appliqué piece and the background fabric. It will fuse to the fabrics when pressed with the iron. (Follow directions that come with the fusable interfacing.) The edges of the appliqué piece may be machine stitched or left unstitched.

There are many possibilities for appliquéing ribbon, cording, leather, novelty fabrics, and trims to your work. Avoid fabrics which will ravel. Also, if washing is a consideration, be sure to use only washable materials. Old appliqué work was done by cutting out floral designs from chintz fabrics. Many exciting printed fabrics may be used this way.

Hawaiian Appliqué

Hawaiian quilts are direct appliquè on a large scale. They began when missionaries from New England went to Hawaii in the early 1800s. The style probably evolved from the art of paper cutting already practiced by many Pennsylvanian missionaries.

Many traditions are connected with the Hawaiian quilt. The quiltmaker's design includes special symbols for the recipient. These messages are conveyed in the colors and motifs on the quilt.

Traditionally, the custom was to never copy another quilter's pattern. When a quilt was washed and hung outside on the line to dry, the right side would be folded in so that the design would not show and could not be copied. However, today, people are allowed to trace patterns to preserve the art of Hawaiian quiltmaking. Traditionally, a quiltmaker would never give a quilt pattern away until the original quilt was completed, otherwise the receiver of the pattern might finish her quilt first.

Taboos are associated with the Hawaiian quilt. Hawaiians will not sit on a bed quilt because the flag is often symbolized on the quilt. Animals and fish are considered unlucky symbols for quilts. As the Hawaiians are people who love the bright colored flowers of their land, floral patterns are the most popular.

This Hawaiian pillow, made by the author, is yellow with red appliqué.

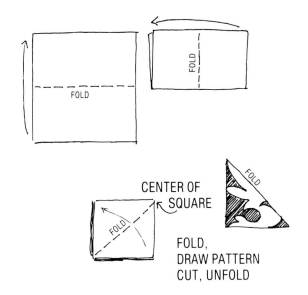

CENTER OF SQUARE

FOLD, DRAW PATTERN CUT, UNFOLD

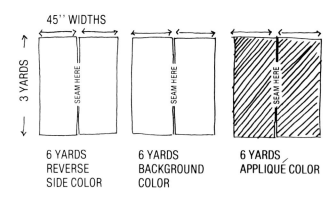

3 YARDS

SEAM HERE

6 YARDS
REVERSE
SIDE COLOR

6 YARDS
BACKGROUND
COLOR

6 YARDS
APPLIQUÉ COLOR

Techniques

When creating an Hawaiian quilt plan on using a sample paper pattern. You may want to cut several sample patterns to get the feel of the way these appliqué patterns are derived. Fold a piece of square paper in half, then in half again, and then fold it on a line from the center to the corner. Draw a design on the paper in the same manner as you would stylize a paper snowflake, carefully planning not to cut too much of the folded area away. Then cut on the drawn line and unfold.

When you design a pattern that pleases you, cut it out in colored paper before you buy quilt fabric. Place the cut design on another piece of colored paper to see how it will look. Try several color arrangements. This will help you visualize before investing in fabric. Usually in Hawaiian quilts the dark fabric is placed on top of the light fabric so the dark will not show through the top appliquéd fabric.

Two large pieces of fabric are needed to make the surface an Hawaiian quilt. One for the top layer is cut in the pattern and is appliquéd to the second or background layer. Sometimes Hawaiian quilts are made from two large bed sheets. The sheets may be dyed to your own color choices. Another way to acquire wide fabric is to buy 45" width yardage and seam the lengths together. This method of course will leave seams on the surface, but they are barely visible after the quilting is completed. One hundred percent cotton fabric is the best for handling and is easier to manage if it has not been washed. You may preshrink your fabric, or you may shrink the fabric after the

appliqué design is complete if both layers are the same type of material. Shrinkage will be equal and there will be no problem.

For a queen or king size bed a total of 18 yards of fabric is needed. This will be sufficient for the top two layers and the reverse side of the quilt. Purchase 6 yards of fabric in one color for the top appliqué piece and 12 yards of fabric in another color for the background and for the reverse side of the quilt. To begin, rip off the selvedges, then cut the fabric in 3-yard lengths. You will have six pieces of yardage. Make three wide pieces of fabric by machine sewing two lengths together. (Sew the same colors together.) Do not open the seams, but keep them closed and press well.

Now, you must transfer your original design to the piece of fabric to be appliquéd. Fold your fabric as you did the sample paper pattern, in half, in half again, then fold once on the bias from the center to the corner. Press the folds with the iron as you go. Enlarge your sample paper pattern to the size of the folded fabric. You are enlarging only one-eighth of the

1. SAMPLE PAPER PATTERN

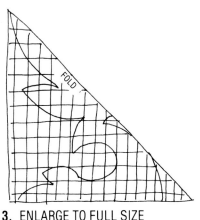

2. TRANSFER TO GRAPH PAPER

3. ENLARGE TO FULL SIZE PAPER PATTERN

Transfer the paper pattern to the folded cloth by drawing around it with a pencil.

Appliqué the top piece down with the appliqué or blindstitch by rolling the edge under with your fingernail as you go. This appliqué technique works very well on a large scale, see the photo at the beginning of this chapter.

When the appliqué is finished, quilt the Hawaiian quilt as you would any other quilt, see chapter 5. The quilting pattern follows the outline of the appliqué design and represents the waves breaking on the shore. The rows are quilted about one finger's width apart.

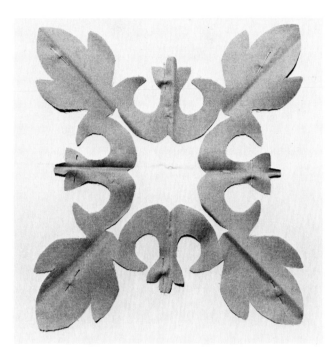

Match up the appliqué piece to the background by matching creases put into both pieces with the iron.

finished design. This can be done on butcher or brown wrapping paper. Mark your paper pattern with the word "fold" on the edge where it will be, see how to enlarge a pattern, this chapter. Cut out the paper pattern and place it on the folded fabric, making sure the fold of the fabric is on the same side as the "fold" of the paper pattern. Pin the pattern to the cloth. With a pencil draw around the outside of the pattern. Remove the paper pattern, pin the layers of cloth together, and cut on the pencil line through all eight thicknesses of fabric. It will be difficult to cut, so make sure you use a good sharp pair of dressmaker shears. The fabric may move around a little while you are cutting, causing some layers to be cut differently than others. Do not be concerned over these differences as the traditional Hawaiian quilts have them. They are unavoidable.

Take the background fabric and fold it as you did the top appliquéd fabric, pressing it as you fold. Then unfold this piece of fabric. Its folds will match those of the cut appliquéd piece. Lay out the background piece of fabric on a large flat area. Place the cut appliquéd piece on top of it, slowly unfold, and match the pressed folds of the two pieces. Even up the fabrics, pin the top to the bottom, and then baste them together about ½" from the raw edges.

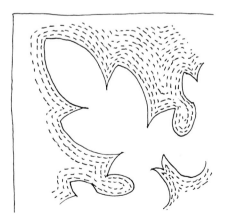

QUILTING PATTERN

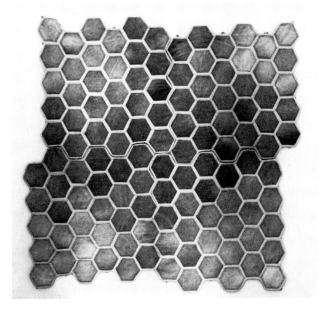

Hanging Quilt II, the author. 56″ × 56″. This hanging quilt is made of four pieces. The used denim hexagons were appliquéd onto cotton knit fabric dyed with pink fiber reactive dyes. This piece was designed to be taken apart and then arranged in various positions which create changes in light and dark patterns and in the shape. There are buttons and loops on the back of the quilt to fasten it together. (above) Detail—front of quilt.

(below) Detail—back of quilt.

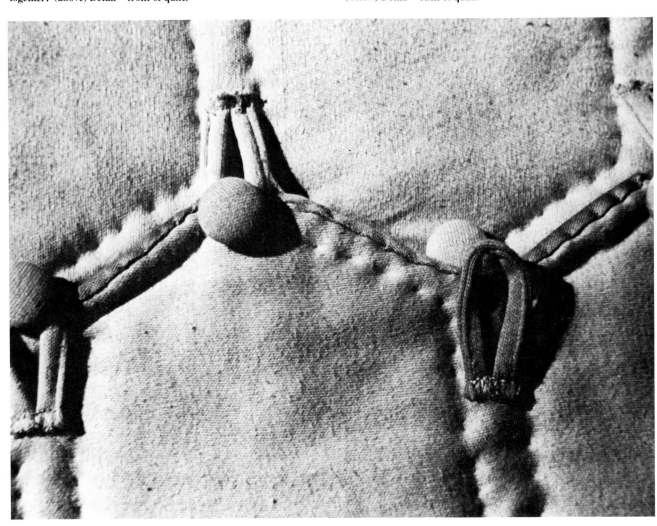

A Section of a Long Skirt, the author. A section of a long skirt that has been appliquéd with pieces of old crocheted lace.

Appliquéd pillow. Cathie Merkel. 21″ × 21″. There is stuffing under the cat which was appliquéd by using the satin stitch on the sewing machine. Many small flowers also were appliquéd by using fancy stitching.

Pat's Robe, Judy Dumm. This is a long vest made for a choir director's robe. It is made from 100 percent cotton hopsacking which was appliquéd with polyester and cotton blends. Before the pieces were machine zig-zagged in place, they were stuffed slightly. Modeled by Jennifer Dumm.

Appliquéd vest, the author. Flowers were cut out of drapery fabric and appliquéd to the printed cotton challis fabric using double sided fusable interfacing. The flowers were then satin stitched around the edges.

Reverse Appliqué

Reverse appliqué is the cutting away of fabric to add color instead of the adding of fabric for color. It is a popular technique today as evidenced by the many molas for sale at stores that carry South and Central American goods. A mola is a reverse appliqué cotton panel which is part of a dress. Today, as they have become a fad, they are being used as wall hangings, mats, pillows, and for clothing.

Molas are a relatively new art form. They have been made for only the past 130 years in Central America. They are believed to have originated from body painting and then fabric painting. Painted fabric strips were used as decorative borders around hems of dresses. Later the decorative work moved to the bodice. Women did the body painting and today make the molas. Designs are taken primarily from the environment—for instance, nature, birds, beasts, people and animals. However, imagination and geometric shapes are also important in the designs. Colors are mostly bright primary colors and black. From two to seven layers of contrasting cloth are used. The cloth may be heavy or lightweight, the older molas are of heavier cloth. Sewing is done with a hemstitch, and decorative embroidery is used seldomly. However, in recent years decorative embroidery to add detail has become more popular.

The cat pattern has been worked out using layers of construction paper to get the "feel" of the layers of fabric.

Techniques

You may construct a mola in one whole piece or work in blocks which may be sewn together later. One technique may be combined with others. However you work, it is absolutely necessary to work out your design on paper first so that you will understand how the layers of cloth go together.

First, draw out a plan on a piece of paper. It must be relatively simple. Decide how many layers of cloth will be needed to carry out your plan. Each layer will be a different color. There are three layers used in the cat illustration. Each is represented by a different type of shading. Imagine cutting away the first layer of cloth to expose the second layer. Now the second layer is cut away to expose the third layer under it. When you have some ideas try them out using layers of construction paper before you use fabrics. This will further your concept of the technique.

Now, place several layers of contrasting cloth on top of each other. Baste them together at the edges, and tack them together at various points within the piece. Draw your design on the fabric either freehand or by tracing your original design. Use dressmaker's carbon or transfer paper. Cut ¼" to the outside of the drawn line to allow for tucking under. Fold the edge of

This mola from Panama measures 21″ by 17″. Its colors are yellow and red, and it is very worn. Collection of the author.

ORIGINAL PLAN

LAYERS
OF CLOTH

1. [////]
2. [   ]
3. [XXXX]

FIRST LAYER
CUT AWAY

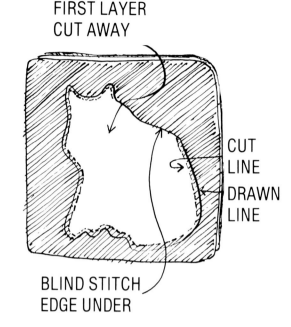

CUT
LINE

DRAWN
LINE

BLIND STITCH
EDGE UNDER

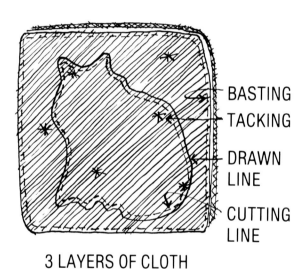

BASTING

TACKING

DRAWN
LINE

CUTTING
LINE

3 LAYERS OF CLOTH

Tips for Good Appliqué

When selecting fabrics, remember that bulky fabrics will cause puckering if used for the appliqué piece and will not lie smoothly if used for the background.

When laying out an appliqué piece on the background fabric, make sure you:

1. Do not force the pieces to fit together by stretching the fabrics.
2. Match up the grains of the fabrics on both layers.

When stitching:

1. Fold or roll back a neat even hem.
2. It is most comfortable to stitch toward yourself on the edge closest to you.
3. Pull the appliqué thread tight as you stitch. This will cause the appliquéd piece to stand out slightly and the stitches to disappear.
4. Ease fabric at the sharp tips and curves, your most difficult stitching areas.
5. Make neat stitches and work evenly with thread of a matching color.

When finishing, do not press the appliqué flat as it will crease.

fabric under as you stitch. When the first layer design has been firmly stitched, repeat the process by tracing the design onto the second layer of fabric. After the second layer of fabric is traced, cut and stitched, repeat again until there are no more layers of fabric.

To vary your work, one part of the design may be cut down to the bottom layer of color, whereas another part may be cut down to the second or third layers exposing a different color. An interesting variation is to use a layer of patterned cloth. If a small area of a new color is desirable, it can be introduced by slipping a small piece of cloth in behind a slit cut in the cloth for the design.

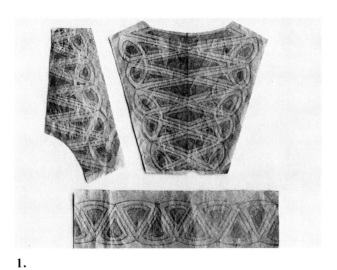

1.

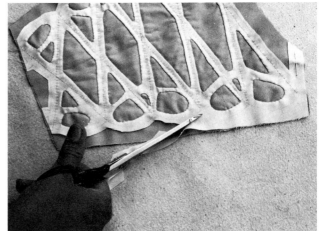

3.

2.

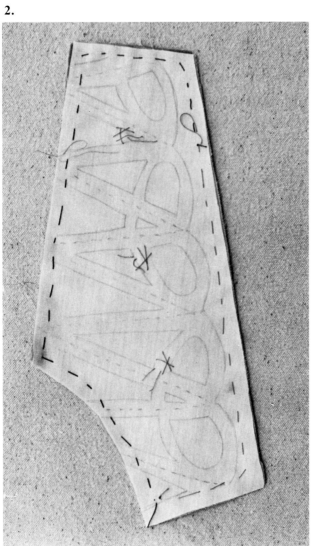

4.

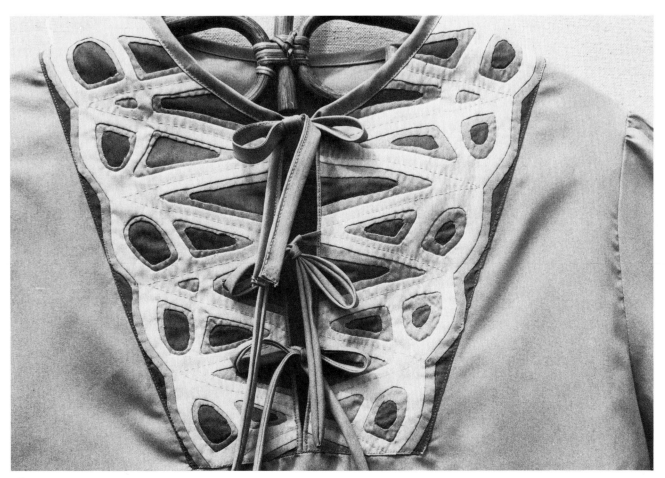

5.

6.

1. Make patterns on wrinkled brown paper after pressing it flat. This makes the paper easy to handle. When drawing designs on the paper, consider how many layers of fabric will be needed and which drawn line represents which layer of fabric. These patterns are for the yoke and cuffs of a blouse.

2. The three layers of fabric needed for this design are joined by basting and tacking. Then the design is transferred from the brown paper to the top layer of fabric by transfer paper.

3. The first layer of fabric is being cut away (about ¼″ beyond the drawn line). As this piece required much cut work, it was not all cut at the same time. Some permanent stitching has been done for ornamental purposes.

4. These finished cuff pieces show all three layers of fabric.

5. Detail.

6. This is the finished blouse.

(above) *Red and White Coverlet*, Brenda Fisk. 90″ × 120″. Unbleached muslin was laid over red cotton broadcloth. The design was worked in reverse appliqué or cutwork. Photograph by Robert Jenkins.

(right) *Mola for Tea*, Linnea Davis. 15″ × 16″. This piece is made from 100 percent cotton fabric in black, red and green, and is done in reverse appliqué technique. Photograph by the artist.

Chapter Four

PIECING

A pieced and appliquéd basket pattern is depicted on U.S. postage stamps of a few years ago.

Whereas appliqué is generally used to join curved pieces of fabric together, piecing designs are generally geometric. While there are some curved-pieced patterns, only the experienced craftsperson should attempt them. Piecing involves the cutting of fabric into many sizes and shapes to be rejoined by sewing.

Developing Patterns

Graph Paper Drafting

In order to design your own pattern or copy one you like, it is essential to understand how basic quilt patterns are structured. Try experimenting with each of the basic ways of drafting a pattern.

As you are sketching, remember how important scale is. An entire quilt may be created from one block or from any number of blocks. Each has a different impact. Experimenting with different sizes of graph paper will give you some idea of the feeling of scale.

Try not to overcomplicate your drafting. For example, you may find that while working on a draft using sixteen squares, it could be done more easily with four squares. Use each block for the purpose of creating a pattern that cannot be reproduced with another block.

After you have done some experimenting, check your understanding of the basic structure of quilt patterns by examining old quilts. See if you can reconstruct their drafts on paper.

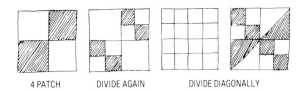

4 PATCH   DIVIDE AGAIN   DIVIDE DIAGONALLY

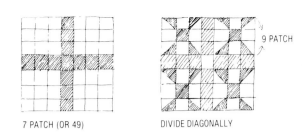

7 PATCH (OR 49)   DIVIDE DIAGONALLY

Four Patch (or Sixteen). A four patch block will be divided into four squares and each square may be divided again to create a total of sixteen squares. Or only two squares may be divided. Further divisions may be drawn diagonally in some or all of the squares. Each of the original four squares may be identical, or two repeat units may be used.

Seven Patch (or Forty-nine). A seven patch block is created when seven squares run horizontally and seven vertically. A vertical and a horizontal band runs through the forty-nine squares. Each corner of the total block is a separate nine patch unit. These squares may be divided diagonally.

Paper Folding

Using a paper folding technique to produce a surface pattern is simple and gives the same results as drafting on graph paper. The difference is that you work with a piece of paper that is the actual size of the finished block—an advantage if you prefer working large. The disadvantage is that paper folding is slower than sketching on graph paper.

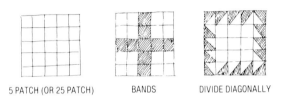

5 PATCH (OR 25 PATCH)   BANDS   DIVIDE DIAGONALLY

Five Patch (or Twenty-five). A five patch block equals twenty-five squares as there are five vertically and five horizontally. Sometimes, but not necessarily, there may be a band running both horizontally and vertically through the center of the five patch block. When several blocks are completed and are joined together, these bands will create an overall lattice effect. Some of the squares may be divided diagonally if desired.

Take a piece of paper (such as typing paper) and cut it approximately 8" to 10" square or a size you prefer. Now fold the paper horizontally, vertically, or diagonally. You will find your paper folding looks like the graph paper drawings previously described.

Try these two examples of paper folding and then do several of your own. Fold the paper in half, then in half again in the same direction. Now in the other direction, fold the paper in half, and in half again. When you open the paper you have a block with sixteen squares. With colored pencils fill in some squares. The paper may be folded again, this time diagonally. When it is opened, fill in some shapes created by the diagonal folding.

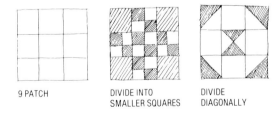

9 PATCH   DIVIDE INTO SMALLER SQUARES   DIVIDE DIAGONALLY

Nine Patch. Three squares run horizontally and three vertically to create a nine patch block. All or some of these squares may be divided diagonally or into smaller squares.

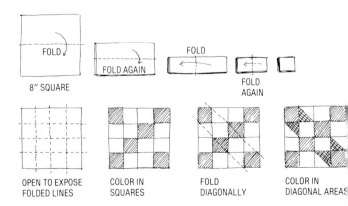

8" SQUARE   FOLD AGAIN   FOLD   FOLD AGAIN

OPEN TO EXPOSE FOLDED LINES   COLOR IN SQUARES   FOLD DIAGONALLY   COLOR IN DIAGONAL AREAS

January II, © Nancy Crow. 80″ × 80″. Machine strip piecing was used to assemble this cotton/polyester fabric. The hand quilting was completed by Velma Brill. Photograph by the artist.

Matisse with Black, © Nancy Crow. 76″ × 76″. Using cotton and polyester blends, this piece was machine pieced using the strip piecing technique and then was hand quilted. The hand quilting was executed by Velma Brill. Photograph by the artist.

Equus Robas II, the author. 65″ × 65″. Inspired by various aspects of costume history, this piece is both a wall hanging and saddle covering for a horse. The material is nylon fabric dyed with dispersed dyes. Transfer printing was done on squares of fabric which were then pieced together on the machine. The piece was then quilted with metallic threads on the sewing machine.

(above) *Sunset Blocks*, Nancy Halpern. 22″ × 32″. Using cottons and blends, this small piece was machine pieced and then hand quilted. Photograph by the artist.

(right) *Counterpoint*, Debra S. Millard. 76″ × 92″. The design has been worked out through exploration of pattern with a computerized weave program. Muslin fabric was dyed with fiber reactive dye to obtain subtle value and hue gradations. It has been machine pieced and hand quilted. Photograph by Tom Allen.

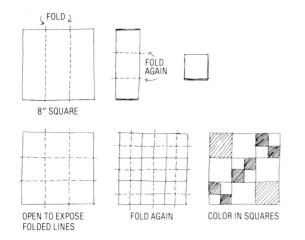

FOLD

FOLD AGAIN

8" SQUARE

OPEN TO EXPOSE
FOLDED LINES

FOLD AGAIN

COLOR IN SQUARES

Fold another square of paper in thirds. Then fold in thirds, folding from the other direction. Open the paper to expose nine squares. Make additional folds, then open the paper and color in the areas desired. Try additional arrangements using your own folding ideas. Work with all diagonal folds as well.

Developing a Surface

When you find a block that pleases you, experiment with your block on graph paper. Using four identical blocks for each sketch, rearrange them in several ways until you find a pleasing arrangement. Then develop this arrangement by carrying out the plan with additional blocks. This approach will help you further understand your block and what it looks like with additional repeats.

Now, decide on the size of the individual block. To determine this size requires two considerations—scale and the size of the finished piece. For example, you may want the size of the finished quilt to be approximately 80" by 90". You could have eight blocks going in one direction and nine in the other. Each block would be 10" square, giving you a small scale and a very busy overall pattern (A). Another option is

to make the blocks twice this size (20" square). Then, only four blocks are needed across and five down. An extra 10" will need to be added to the length of the quilt to keep the blocks square (B). The overall scale will not be as busy, and this may be the best way to present your block. You may think fewer blocks would be easier and faster to complete, but consider that you may lose something of the feeling of the block and its repeat pattern if it is too large. On the other hand, a large block may be the better choice. Take time to sketch on graph paper what the scale will be in order to get an idea of the impact of the design.

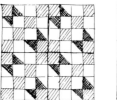

DIFFERENT ARRANGEMENTS USING ONE BLOCK

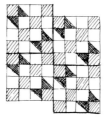

DEVELOP AN ARRANGEMENT WITH
ADDITIONAL BLOCKS

DIFFERENT ARRANGEMENTS USING ONE BASIC BLOCK

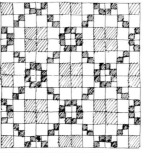

DEVELOP AN ARRANGEMENT
WITH ADDITIONAL BLOCKS

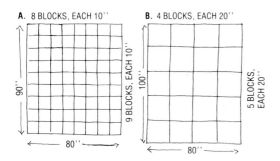

A. 8 BLOCKS, EACH 10"   B. 4 BLOCKS, EACH 20"

90"

9 BLOCKS, EACH 10"

100"

5 BLOCKS, EACH 20"

80"

80"

Preparation and Working with Fabric

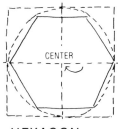

RIGHT ANGLE TRIANGLE MADE FROM A SQUARE

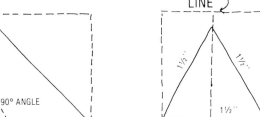

EQUILATERAL TRIANGLE MADE FROM A SQUARE

HEXAGON
1. DRAW SQUARE
2. DIVIDE INTO FOUR EQUAL SQUARES
3. DRAW CIRCLE
4. SIDES OF HEX-AGON EQUAL THE RADIUS

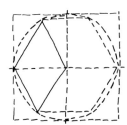

A **DIAMOND** HAS FOUR EQUAL SIDES
1. FOLLOW STEPS FOR HEXAGON
2. LINES FROM THE CENTER DRAWN TO THE CORNERS EQUAL SIDES & RADIUS

OPPOSITE SIDES ARE EQUAL ON A **RHOMBOID**
1. DRAW A RECTANGLE
2. CONNECT LINES FROM CORNERS TO OPPOSITE SIDES

Making Templates

A template is a tool that you can make or purchase. If you want special sizes for your own design you will need to make your own.

Once you develop the surface design of your quilt, you may prepare to cut the fabric. Draw your block out on paper in the desired size. Count the shapes in this block. For example, the first block illustrated in Paper Folding has two basic shapes, a square and a triangle. There are twelve squares and eight triangles. Since all the squares, like all the triangles, are of equal size, only one template is needed for each shape. If this block had a square or a triangle of a different size, an additional template would be needed for that size.

Make templates accurately. An error of 1/8" may not seem like much when considering a 3" square, but when multiplied times the length of the quilt, it will cause poor fitting. Use cardboard for the templates. With use lighter cardboard will need replacing more quickly than heavier, but it may be cut with scissors. Heavier cardboard must be cut with an X-acto or mat knife. Choose the cardboard which best suits your purpose.

For each shape two templates should be cut, one including a 1/4" seam allowance, the other no seam allowance. In the size needed, draw the basic shapes for your design on the cardboard. They may be drawn as in the illustration. Then, carefully cut out the cardboard shapes.

Marking and Cutting the Fabric

Prepare the fabric by preshrinking and pressing it well. If it is off grain, stretch and press it back into shape. Also, check to see if the fabric has a *nap,* a surface texture, as it will affect the surface of the quilt and may become a design element of which to take advantage. Corduroy, for example, has a raised nap which appears to have two distinct values when viewed from different angles. Decide now whether you will machine or hand stitch your quilt together because there are two ways to mark your fabric.

Carefully mark the cutting line and the seam line.

Mark your fabric for hand stitching by using the larger template that includes the seam allowance. Mark the total number of pieces and types of fabric needed on top of each template so that you will know how many to cut. For example, the total number may be twenty, including ten blue and ten white pieces. Place the template on the wrong side of the fabric and trace around the shape with a sharp-pointed pencil to give a crisp, clean line. Make sure you work with the grain of the fabric while fitting the shapes together to get the most from the fabric. After marking the cutting edge of the shape with the larger template, mark the seam line of the shape with the smaller template.

In some cases, you may wish to dispense with templates and draw directly on to the fabric. In this case, a ruler and yardstick may be used to draw the simpler geometric shapes, such as squares and rectangles. Simply measure and draw the shape on the fabric and then draw an additional ¼" seam allowance. The more complicated patterns, such as the hexagon, should be drawn with a template. Again, absolute precision is needed when drawing on the fabric.

Mark the fabric for machine stitching as you did for hand stitching. However, in this case a seam line is not needed because you will use the sewing machine guides for seam allowances. Simply mark the cutting line as directed in the previous instructions.

With great accuracy, cut the pieces of fabric. Store them with "like" shapes together while keeping them flat. This will facilitate work when you begin to assemble the pieces.

Sewing the Pieces Together

The assembly for each pattern will be different. Do it the way that seems the most logical. Trust your common sense to show you the easiest and fastest way. To make assembly easier, sew as many seams as possible in a straight line trying to avoid sewing into corners at difficult angles. Again, accuracy is all important. All the pieces of the fabric *must* be matched and sewn together by hand or by machine with great care.

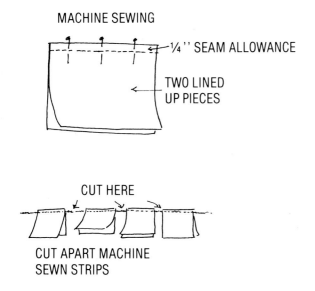

When machine assembling, place the right sides of the fabric together and carefully line up the edges. If the stitching line is to be long, use a few pins to keep it from sliding. Carefully stitch together using a ¼" seam allowance. Use the gauge on the sewing machine to guide you. Handle the sewing process like an assembly line. After each sewing is complete, do not break off the bobbin and surface thread, simply slide two more fabric pieces under the machine's presser foot and sew again. Of course, you must pull the threads out about 2" or 3" between each sewing. This assembly line technique will save a great deal of time. When you finish sewing, remove the long string of sewn pieces from the machine and cut them apart.

Sew the smaller pieces together before sewing them to the larger ones (A). For greatest speed, sew them together in one strip (B and C). Then sew the strips together to form the block (D). The finished

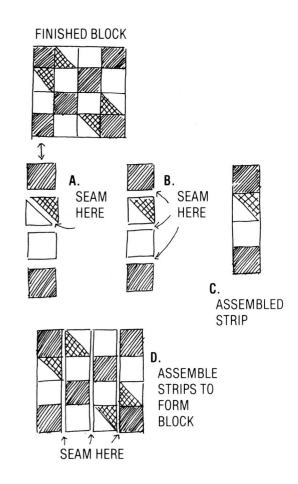

blocks are then assembled to create the entire quilt by sewing them in strips and then sewing these strips together. Pieces should always be pinned together where the seams meet so that they will meet perfectly when sewn.

To make seams match perfectly when sewn, it is a good idea to pin the seams before stitching.

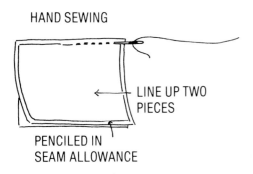

HAND SEWING

LINE UP TWO PIECES

PENCILED IN SEAM ALLOWANCE

Paper hexagons have been basted down, and now the pieces of fabric are being whipped together.

Assembly is the same for hand sewing as for machine sewing only you use a tiny and even running stitch to put the pieces together. The penciled-in seam line will guide you. Begin and end each sewn line with a small knot or a backstitch. Load a #10 sharp needle with as many stitches as possible before pulling it through the fabric. Use cotton thread if possible or cotton-wrapped polyester thread. Some threads will twist and knot up while being worked by hand. Avoid this by using short threads that you have coated with beeswax.

If you are making an entire quilt out of one shape, such as a hexagon, the following method of assembly is the easiest and most accurate. Using a lightweight paper, such as typing paper, trace and cut out several shapes using a template of the finished size (no seam allowance). Baste these pieces of paper to the wrong side of the fabric pieces which were cut to include the seam allowance. Assemble the basted pieces by placing the right sides of these shapes together and whip them together permanently with small stitches. When a shape is surrounded by other shapes, the paper may be removed by cutting the basting thread. It may be used again.

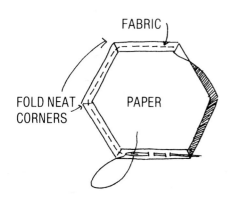

FABRIC

FOLD NEAT CORNERS

PAPER

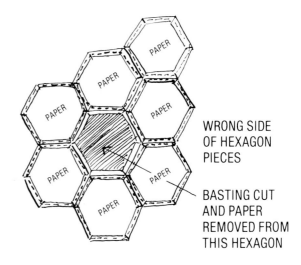

PAPER

WRONG SIDE OF HEXAGON PIECES

BASTING CUT AND PAPER REMOVED FROM THIS HEXAGON

As you are working, press often. Seams are pressed in one direction. Do not open a seam to press it as the seam will weaken. It is also difficult to open and press down a ¼" seam. It is a good idea to press all the seams in the same direction if possible. But when a combination of dark and light colors are used (usually the case), press the seams under the dark fabric so they will not show through the lighter fabric.

Borders

An important consideration is how you want to finish your quilt. Your surface design and finish should compliment one another. Several options are available—applying bias strips to the edges, using a self-binding technique, and adding borders, see chapter 6.

A *border* is often added to quilts as a kind of frame. There are as many ways to border a quilt as there are people making quilts. Remember that since it both frames and encloses the overall surface pattern, it affects the total look.

A border may be planned as you are working on the surface design of the quilt itself or after you complete the quilt. It may be wide or thin, plain or patterned. Whatever you choose, the only requirement is that it compliment the quilt pattern. This may be a great place for innovation! Remember too that the edges and borders of a quilt do not have to be straight edged.

For ease in construction, when cutting and piecing a pattern for the border, cut the pieces in the same proportions as you cut the quilt itself. This act does not preclude making the border pattern larger or smaller than that of the quilt. For example, the block pattern for your quilt may be 12″ square. If you wish to have a border of the same pattern, only smaller, base your border design on a 6″ square. This will create a smaller pattern and will add interest to the quilt; at the same time the quilt and border will piece together easily.

Borders often are added after the quilt surface itself is put together. The borders are cut and pieced in strips, then laid out alongside the quilt surface, and are sewn last onto the quilt top.

Designs and Techniques

Log Cabin

This fast, easy technique does not require templates. The charm of the log cabin block is the variety of ways in which the blocks may be arranged. This is because one side of the block is made with strips of light fabrics and the other with strips of dark fabrics. The fabrics may be identical on each side, or there may be a variety of dark fabrics on the dark side and a variety of light fabrics on the light side. This contrast creates many arrangements for the log cabin blocks. When trying out this block, make at least four to eight blocks to allow for experimenting with various arrangements.

This back side of a log cabin square shows the dark on one half and the light on the other.

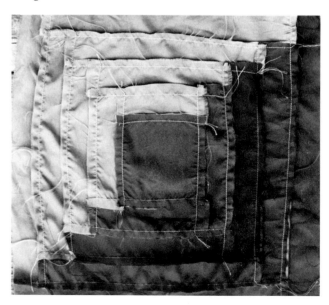

SEW ON SIDES FIRST

SEW ON TOP & BOTTOM SECOND

6″ BLOCK

12″ BLOCK

Cut two lengths of fabric, one dark and one light. Each should be 1½″ wide. The ½″ is the seam allowance for a ¼″ seam on each side of the length. It will take about 100″ in length of fabric to make a 9″ finished log cabin square. There will be about 50″ of dark fabric and about 50″ of light fabric. These lengths do not all have to be from one strip of fabric. Use shorter strips since they are cut as work progresses. Start by cutting a 1½″ piece off one of the long strips. This is the center of the log cabin square and may be either the dark or light fabric, although it is traditionally dark. The first strip of fabric (dark or light) to be attached is laid along the right side of the center square and stitched on the machine with a ¼″ seam allowance, using the gauge on the sewing machine (A). Press this first strip back and then cut it off evenly with the bottom of the center square (B). If the first strip of fabric was light, the second strip should also be light; if the first strip was dark, the second strip should also be dark. Attach this second strip by placing it alongside the bottom of the center square and the first strip. Sew ¼″ seam allowance (C). Press it back and cut it off evenly with the left side of the center square (D). The third strip should be a change from light to dark fabric or dark to light fabric,

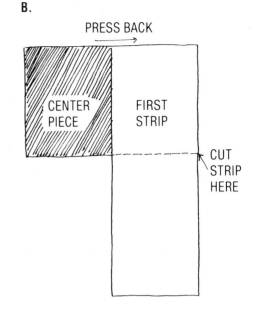

B.

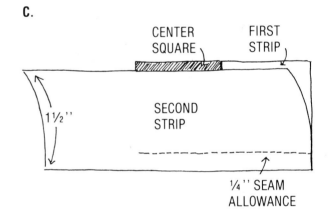

C.

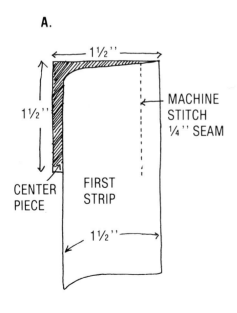

A.

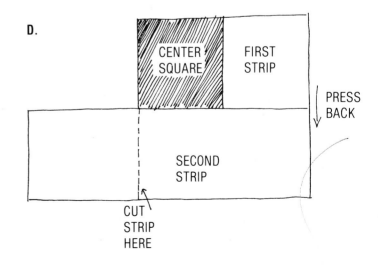

D.

whichever is the case. Lay the third strip along the left side of the center square and second strip, and sew in place (E). Press it back and cut it off evenly with the bottom of the second strip (F). The fourth strip to be sewn is the same as the third. It is sewn along the top of the center square, first and third strips (G). Again, press it back and cut it off evenly with the side of the third strip (H). Continue to sew on strips in a clockwise direction, maintaining the dark and light positions. If four strips are sewn onto each side of the center square, the finished log cabin square will be 9″ square.

After making a few (four to eight) log cabin squares, experiment with them. Move them around on your work table to discover the many dark and light patterns that may be arranged.

E.

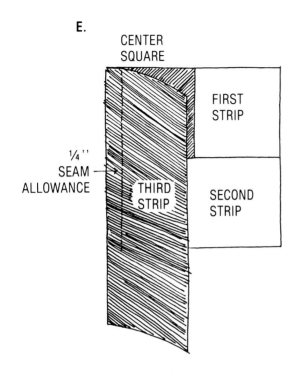

G.

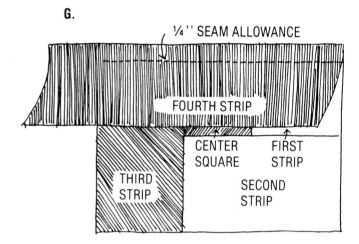

F.

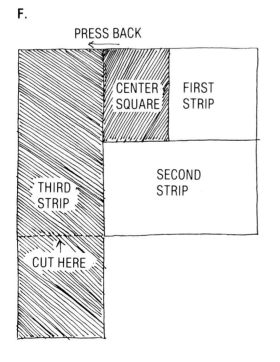

H.

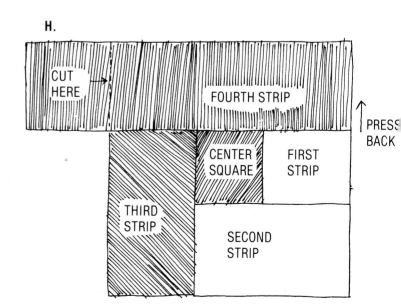

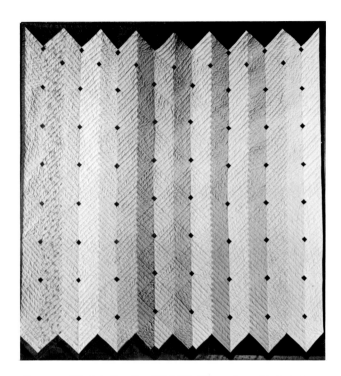

Fences—, Virginia Randles. 78″ × 82″. Using a log cabin technique, this piece was constructed of cotton/polyester fabrics. Hand quilting was executed by Bertha Mast. Photograph by Darrel Tom.

Log cabin quilt, artist unknown. 65″ × 65″. Although this is believed to be a 19th century quilt, the bold colors and design give it a freshness that makes it look contemporary. Courtesy of Bernice Foster. Photograph by Erika Wade.

Log cabin quilt (detail).

Prayer Rug, Shirley Frost. 33″ × 77″. This wall quilt was inspired by an unrequited desire for a Persian rug. It was made of cotton blends, machine pieced, and hand quilted. Photograph by the artist.

Concept of Western Space ©, Shirley Frost. 67″ × 67″. Based on the traditional block called *Road to California*, this wall hanging was made with unbleached muslin and cotton prints in earth tones. The piecing was done by machine and the quilting by hand. Photograph by the artist.

A spider web strip quilt, by the author. 5'9" × 7'. A dark blue print was purchased for the star shapes, but the "spiderwebs" were made from fabric scraps. The quilt is backed with fake fur.

Earth, Water, Air and Fire, **Radka Donnell. 82″ × 98″. Until 1965 Radka was a painter. This is evident in the layout and piecing of the quilt. Cottons and cotton blends were machine pieced. The machine quilting was done by Claire Mielke. Photograph by Tresch & Wenger, Zurich, Switzerland.**

Strip Piecing

One of the easiest, fastest, and most enjoyable piecing techniques is *strip piecing*. The technique may be used to create any shape desired. It is fun to do and uses up small bits of leftover fabric. After trying the few shapes suggested here, try shapes of your own. This technique is very versatile and may be adapted easily.

Spider Web. Cut several pieces of paper 12″ square. The paper you use should be typing or butcher paper weight. If you plan to make a bed quilt, figure how many squares you will need to make it. You may make the squares a little larger or smaller than 12″.

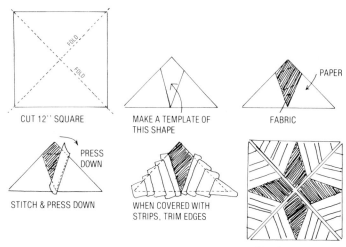

CUT 12″ SQUARE

MAKE A TEMPLATE OF THIS SHAPE

PAPER

FABRIC

PRESS DOWN

STITCH & PRESS DOWN

WHEN COVERED WITH STRIPS, TRIM EDGES

SEW FOUR TOGETHER

Fold a square of paper diagonally and then fold it diagonally again. Unfold it. The result is four triangles. Cut out each triangle. Draw a diamond shape on one of the triangles by marking the center of the triangle's base and by drawing equidistant lines to the other two sides of the triangle. Cut out this small shape. You will need to make a cardboard template of it as it will be your guide for cutting many pieces of fabric.

With this small diamond shaped guide, mark several diamonds on cloth and cut them out. (You are not marking or cutting seam allowances.) Traditionally, this shape is cut from dark fabric. These pieces must all be of the same fabric regardless of whether you follow tradition and they must contrast with the strips in order to create the pattern.

Now, take one of your diamond shaped pieces of fabric and pin it to a triangular piece of paper as in the illustration. Then, stitch about five fabric strips of varying widths on each side of the diamond shape. Stitch directly on the paper with a small machine stitch allowing about ¼″ seams. The width of the strips used depends upon the overall size with which you are working. Larger sizes will require wider strips, small ones, narrower strips. Place the first strip right side down on the fabric shape, stitch on the edge, and press it out. Continue adding strips by stitching and pressing so the next strip will always be stitched on the preceding one.

When the paper triangle is covered with strips, trim the edges of the strips using the paper as a guide. Rip the paper off the back of the fabric carefully. Be careful on the edges or you may rip out the stitching.

Sew four of these triangular shapes together and you have created one block. When several blocks are sewn together, you will see the spider web pattern emerge.

Eight Point Star. The eight point star shape may be any size you wish. Make your pattern on paper for one-eighth of the star by creating a diamond shape. The diamond must have 45° angles at the ends, and all four sides must be equal in length. Cut eight of these diamond shapes out of paper.

Cover them with strips of fabric in the same manner as the spider web design. The colors of the fabric strips may create a pattern. Try covering one end of the diamond shapes with light fabrics and the other with dark. Then, when sewing the star together, sew

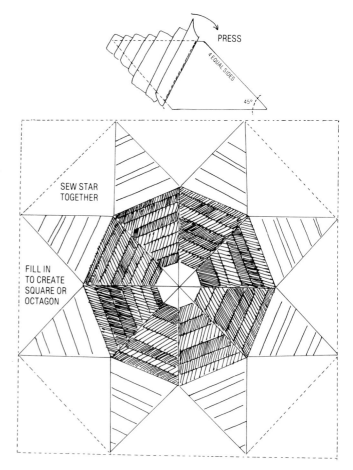

all the light or dark sides together. Specific areas like the center may also contrast. When completely covered, trim the fabric edges to conform to the pattern, and remove the paper pattern.

Sew the star together. You may want the finished edge to be this star shape or you may want to enclose it in an octagon or square shape. Measure, cut to fit, and sew in extra pieces. Measuring is easy as the areas between the points of the star are right angles. Lay the extra piece along one side of a star point, right sides together, pin and sew it in place. Press the extra piece over so it will fill in the space between the two points. Now sew along the other side.

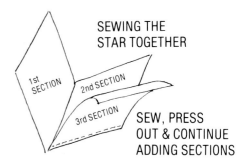

ENCLOSING OUTSIDE OF STAR

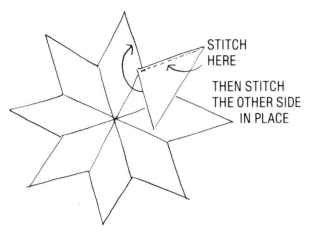

STITCH
HERE

THEN STITCH
THE OTHER SIDE
IN PLACE

STRIP OF CONTRASTING
FABRIC

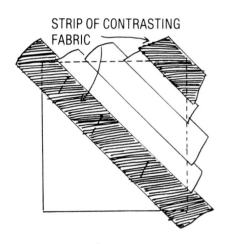

SEW TOGETHER TO CREATE SQUARES

Square. Cut squares of paper the size you need for your project. Pin a strip of fabric from corner to corner. The strip should contrast with the rest of the fabrics you will use on the square. Cover the remaining paper

with fabric strips, trim, and remove paper as shown in the spider web design. The last strip used in the corner of the square should match the contrasting strip used in the center. In succeeding squares, use the same widths of contrasting fabric in the center and corner. To finish, sew squares together, matching up the contrasting strips to form squares.

Quilt-As-You-Go. A very exciting way to do strip piecing is to quilt it as you go. This technique may be used on any of the shapes discussed here as well as on any you might devise. It adapts very easily to clothing patterns. However, if you are making clothing you must make an allowance for the fabric that will be drawn in by quilting. The only way to gauge this accurately is to make a small sample and measure it before and after quilting.

Cut a piece of fabric the required size for the backing. Lay it right side down on the table. Lay a piece of batting on the backing that is ½" smaller all around.

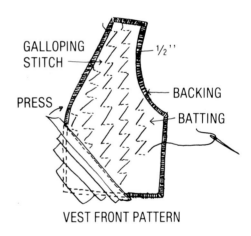

GALLOPING
STITCH

½"

PRESS

BACKING

BATTING

VEST FRONT PATTERN

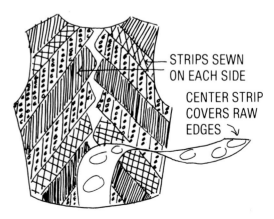

STRIPS SEWN
ON EACH SIDE

CENTER STRIP
COVERS RAW
EDGES

VEST BACK PATTERN

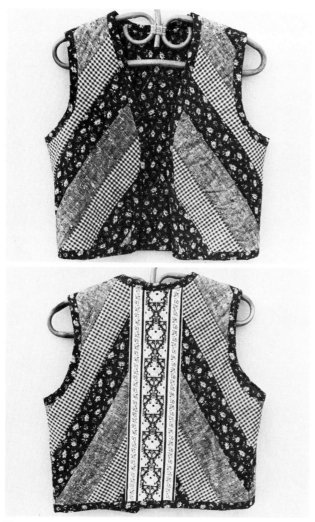

The vest in the photographs above was made by the author according to the illustration on page 49.

The back of a vest by Judy Dumm. This was made using the strip piecing technique plus some hand appliqué.

Vest, Sara Finley. The vest, worn by Andy Finley, was pieced using small squares of denim. It has a fake fur lining.

This extra ½″ on the backing will be the seam allowance when sewing the pre-quilted pieces together later. Do a galloping stitch to fasten batting to the backing; this will keep the two layers from slipping apart. Galloping stitches are a type of basting that hold more securely than a straight line of basting. With threaded needle make continuous rows of Z angle stitches, see illustration.

Now, lay your strips down one at a time and sew them on as you have done before. You may start sewing strips in the center or at one end, as you wish. Press the strips back very quickly. Use a cool iron as you do not want to flatten the batting. All three layers are completed at one time—the pieced or top layer, the batting, and the backing are all stitched into place. For putting the finished "quilt-as-you-go" pieces together, see chapter 5.

The vest pictured was constructed as in the illustration. The front and back of the vest were covered with strips that started at their corners. On the back of the vest the strips were sewn, leaving the center area unfinished, which was later covered by another strip to finish it. After the completed front and back pieces were sewn together, the outside edges were finished with bias tapes, see chapter 5.

Seminole type piecing was used to make this pillow by the author. See illustration on how it was done.

Seminole Piecing

Since the beginning of this century when the Florida Seminole Indians acquired sewing machines, they have created beautiful and colorful patchwork cloth. The cloth is used for jackets, skirts, shirts, and capes. Narrow bands are made to border a skirt, or entire pieces of fabric are made to construct a man's jacket.

Seminole cloth may be created by using a variety of intense color combinations or by selecting pastel fabrics. Small prints may be used. Fabrics with dull or shiny surfaces may add variety also. There are many ways to create special interest with your Seminole piecing. Try using bias tapes and ribbons topstitched onto another piece of fabric. The Seminoles apply rickrack to their strips in a very effective manner. Decorative embroidery by machine or by hand may be interesting. The bias cut of the finished pieces allows for their shaping. Strips may be pieced for garments and eased around armholes and neckbands. You may think of several other ways to develop an interesting cloth.

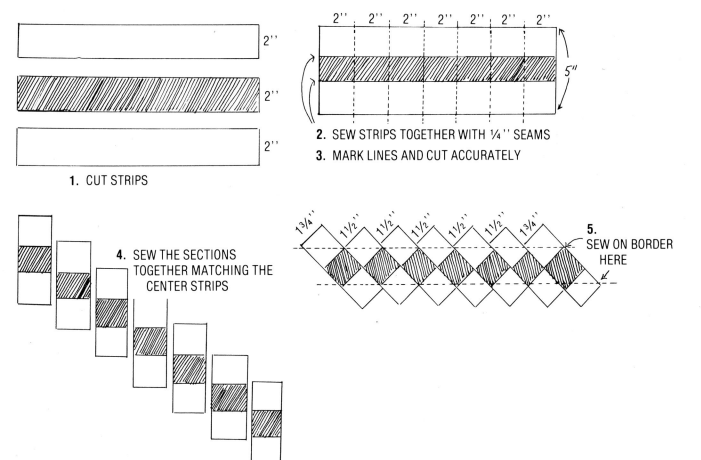

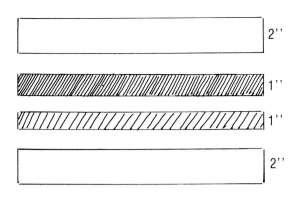
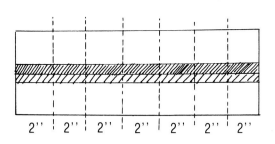

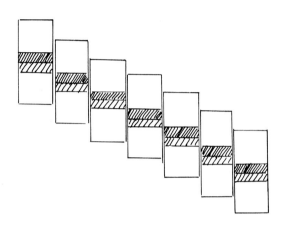
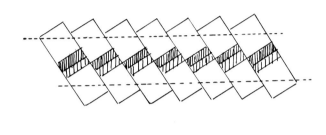

Careful selection of fabrics before beginning is a must for an effective piece of completed cloth. When selecting cloth remember that this technique requires much cutting so it is advisable to use fabrics that are easy to cut. Using sturdy fabrics will aid in keeping an overall firm feel to the finished piece and will discourage raveling. When selecting a variety of fabrics, choose all of a similar weight to create an even "handle" to the finished fabric. For your first project, use fabric that is very easy to handle. The best is 100 percent cotton which must be preshrunk.

With a long straightedge (yardstick or other strip of wood or metal), mark your well pressed fabric with a pencil. Marking the length of the strips to be cut across the width (or weft) of the fabric is convenient. You will need to mark only the cutting lines. The width of the individual strip is of your own choice (depending upon your needs). But, since you use ¼" seam allowances on both sides, you will lose ½" of the width to seams. So, add ½" to the desired width. It speeds up your work to mark several strips at one time. As the fabric is cut and sewn more than once, it is important to measure and mark very carefully.

Cut your strips if you are using a fabric that will be distorted by tearing. Then, put right sides together and sew ¼" seam allowances. Sew with great accuracy. As the seam lines will be cut, use a fairly small stitch. Then, press the sewn fabric. Apply the steam iron to the wrong side of the fabric and, as a general rule, press all the seams in one direction. On occasion, however, they will want to fall in other directions. Do what seems most advantageous at the time.

Now, the sewn strips will be cut into smaller sections. Mark the strip where it is to be cut with a pencil and a ruler. Mark very accurately, then cut exactly on the line.

Sew the sections together according to the pattern you are using. Instead of sewing each individual section and then breaking the thread, slide the second section to be sewn under the sewing foot of the sewing machine. Sew pairs together at one time, then clip them apart and sew all these pairs together for the finished band of cloth. This technique is much faster and saves thread. Press well.

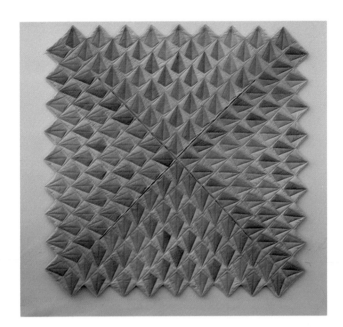

Spike Quilt, the author. 74″ × 74″. Unbleached muslin has been dyed three values of pink with fiber reactive dyes. Small squares of this fabric are then airbrushed with blue spikes. The piece is machine pieced and hand quilted. The center opening where the quilt is not sewn together is left to suggest that the quilt might come apart. Photograph by the artist.

Spike Quilt, Detail.

(above) *Spectrum III* (detail), Virginia Randles. 66″ × 77″. This piece was constructed of polyester and cotton broadcloth and was quilted with 100 percent polyester batting. The hand quilting was executed by Bertha Mast. Photograph by Leland Randles.

(right) *Moonlit Landscape*, Sharon Sharp. 93″ × 78″. This quilt, made of cottons and cotton blends, was machine pieced and hand quilted. Photograph by Alf Photography.

At this time the band may be bordered with a solid piece of cloth or sewn to another Seminole band. It is quite effective to put several Seminole bands together with a strip of plain cloth between them. They could be put into yokes, made into shirt cuffs, or used on a quilt. The possibilities are limitless.

The following patterns are given as examples. You may feel comfortable copying the patterns to learn the basic techniques. But, as you begin, you will notice that many combinations of colors and dimensions will be exciting together. You may begin to copy a design and finish with a final piece of cloth much different than expected. Let your imagination go!

The bottom sample piece of Seminole piecing was constructed in a manner similar to the directions in the illustration on page 52.

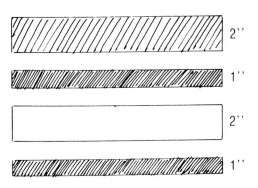

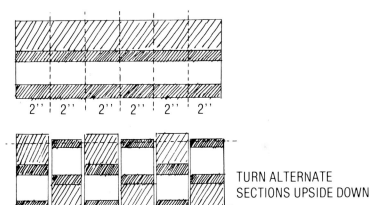

TURN ALTERNATE SECTIONS UPSIDE DOWN

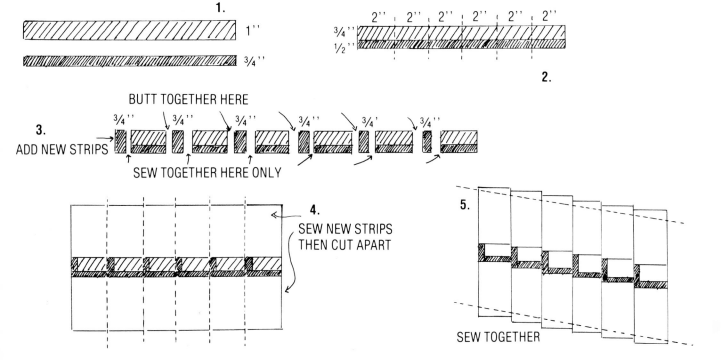

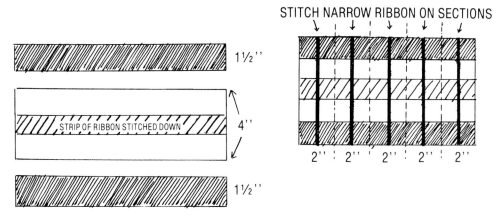

STITCH NARROW RIBBON ON SECTIONS

1½''

STRIP OF RIBBON STITCHED DOWN 4''

1½''

2'' | 2'' | 2'' | 2'' | 2''

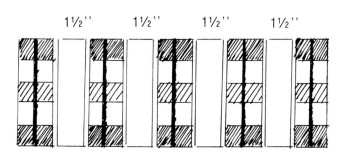

1½''   1½''   1½''   1½''

SEW TOGETHER ALTERNATING WITH NEW STRIPS

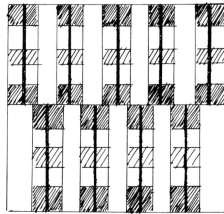

SEW TWO BANDS TOGETHER

This sample was constructed exactly as in the illustration.

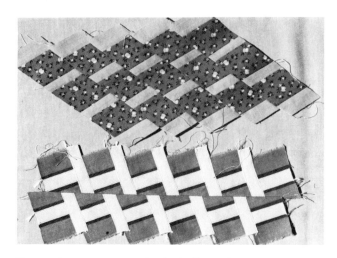

The top piece was constructed as in the illustration.

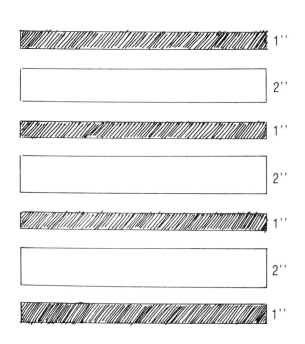

1''

2''

1''

2''

1''

2''

1''

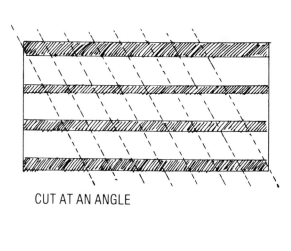

CUT AT AN ANGLE

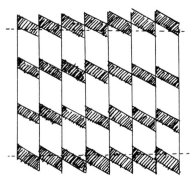

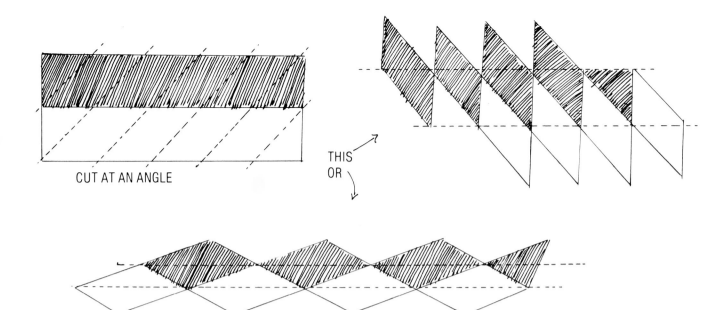

CUT AT AN ANGLE

THIS
OR

These pieces are made similarly to the one in the illustration.

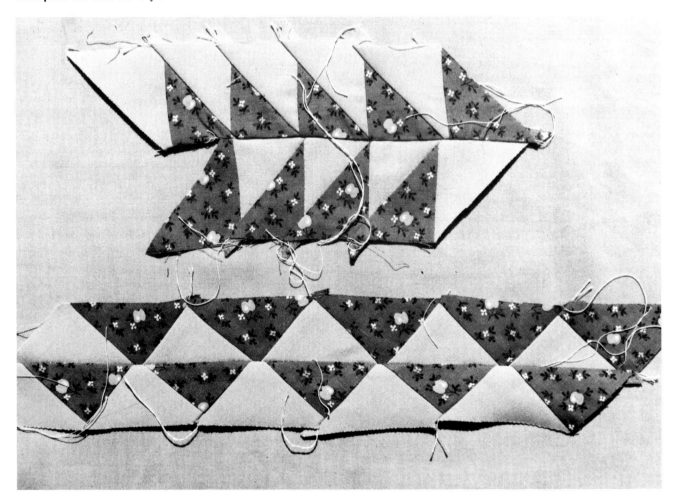

One-half inch strips are taped together horizontally in two different combinations: dark, light, dark; and light, dark, light. Cut ½″ sections from each and join them in blocks alternating them in such a way as to create a checkerboard effect. Groups of blocks may be combined with a plain block for a change of pattern.

Several dark and light ½″ strips are taped together horizontally, starting with a light strip and ending with a dark strip. Then they are cut vertically into ½″ sections. The sections are then retaped by reversing the order; first dark at the top, then light at the top.

One-half inch strips are taped, cut, and reset at an angle.

"Cut and Sew" Piecing Ideas. Take the Seminole piecing principle a step further. There is no need to confine this exciting technique of "cut and sew" to the traditional Seminole styling. It can be adapted to speed up the construction of many quilt patterns. However, although this technique is fast, it still requires great accuracy. If you speed through the construction of a quilt and do a careless job, you will destroy the impact of its design.

When you have a design for a quilt that you wish to construct, first break the overall pattern down on graph paper. Do it as in the pattern drafting section. Start by dissecting the basic block. When you understand its construction, experiment with strips of colored paper. Construction paper is a cheap substitute for fabric, easy to handle, and is worked on a small scale. Cut several strips of paper (½″ wide) in various colors and tape them together horizontally.

Then cut them apart in vertical sections at ½″ intervals, rearrange and retape them. Now, try experimenting by cutting sections at different widths and angles before rearranging and retaping them. The design possibilities are endless. You need not start with a design at all; just move the vertically cut sections of paper around to discover the designs which occur.

After you have worked out your design with paper strips, use your fabric. It should be prepared as you would prepare fabric for any other technique. Use a pencil and a yardstick to mark your strips for cutting. Add ½″ extra on the strip width to give a ¼″ seam allowance on each side of the strip. If your fabric is a type, such as 100 percent cotton, that may be ripped, you may rip the strips without curling and snagging the edges. Because other fabrics create problems when ripped, cut them accurately with scissors.

1.

2.

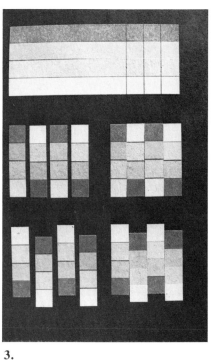

3.

4.

5.

1-3. Four colors are attached in strips, cut vertically and rearranged in a variety of ways.

4. Some sections at the top are cut at an angle while others are cut straight. The two are then attached. The middle and bottom examples show sections cut at an angle and reset with a thin strip of contrasting paper in between.

5. Six strips are attached, cut at an angle, and then reset.

6. An eight point star is created by setting five strips and then cutting them at an angle to reset them.

6.

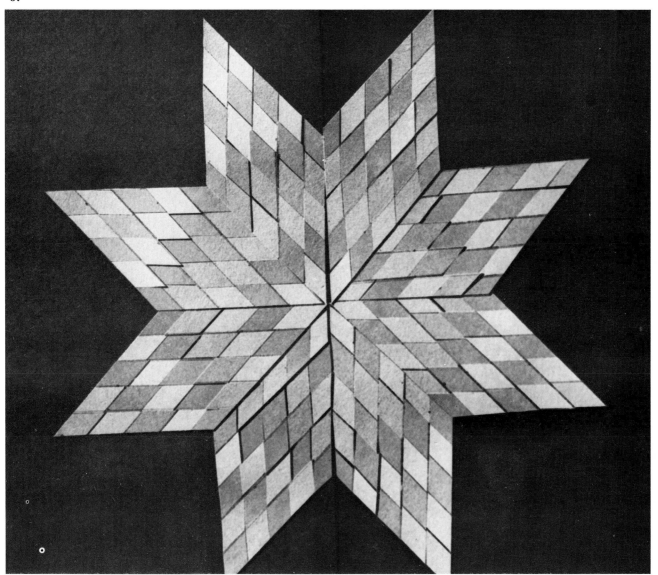

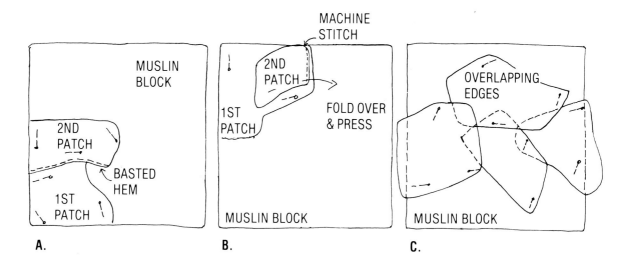

A.

B.

C.

Crazy Quilts

Crazy quilts are made from patches of scrap fabric of any size and shape; no fabric need go to waste. Traditionally, elegant fabrics such as satins, brocades, and velvets were used in making crazy quilts. The quilts were decorated with fancy embroidery stitches over the edges of the patches, and often designs were stitched in the middle of the patches themselves. Sometimes old crazy quilts even had small paintings on them.

The crazy quilt is made in blocks as are pieced quilts. The assorted patches of fabric are arranged on blocks of muslin, each cut about 12″ to 15″ square. Begin by cutting several pieces of muslin so that when sewn together, they will make the desired finished size.

In a corner of a muslin block, place a patch of fabric which has been cut with a right angle. Pin it in place. Add the second patch by first making a small basted hem on one of its edges and then placing it so it will overlap the first patch. Pin it in place. Repeat with more patches of fabric. Basted hems are made only where the edges of a patch will be left exposed. When patches cover the muslin completely, trim them evenly with the edges of muslin. Then, go over the basted areas with fancy embroidery stitches in threads of contrasting colors, see chapter 3 for suggested hand stitches. The basted hems may then be removed.

You may also attach patches on the sewing machine. Start again with a piece cut to fit the corner of the muslin block. Place the second piece on top of the first, with the right sides of the fabric together. Machine stitch along one edge. Then fold the second patch over into place on the muslin and press with the iron. Place more pieces in the same way, where they fit best, always covering the raw edges of one piece with the hemmed edge of the next. Some cutting may be necessary for fit. After working a while, you will soon understand how to manipulate the pieces to take advantage of their size, shape, and color. When the muslin is covered with patches, trim them evenly with the edges of the muslin and decorate the seam lines with embroidery stitches.

Another method of making a crazy quilt is to make it without hems. Patches are arranged (without hems) to overlap each other and to cover the muslin block. Then they are pinned in place. The exposed edges may be covered with hand embroidered stitches or with the zig-zag stitch on the sewing machine.

Crazy quilt handbag by the author. 10½″ × 11½″. Pieces of velveteen, velour, and acrylic were used in this handbag. The flap used trapunto and is outlined with feathers.

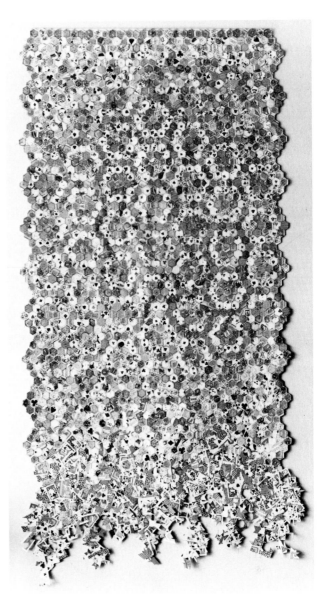

Disintegration—Grandma Can't Put Blocks Together Anymore, Pat Hickman. 84″ × 54″. This hand stitched piece is made of playing cards, gut (hog) sausage casings, and space dyed threads. Photograph by the artist.

The crazy quilt patches may be stuffed as they are sewn into place. When applying each patch, stuff a little batting under it before sewing it down permanently. This will give each piece a "puffy" look. When you finish the crazy quilt top, it will be already quilted and may not need any more batting.

Because of the thickness and busy pattern of the crazy quilt, it should be tied instead of worked in a quilted pattern. It is backed with a lining material, and batting is "sandwiched" between the two layers, see Tying in chapter 5.

Many Victorian crazy quilts have no tying and many have no batt. They were purely decorative quilts, probably not made with any intention of daily use or warmth.

Disintegration—Grandma Can't Put Blocks Together Anymore, **Detail.**

Equus Robas II, the author. 65″ × 65″. This piece is a wall hanging and saddle covering for a horse. It was inspired by various aspects of costume history. The material is nylon fabric dyed with dispersed dyes. Transfer printing was done on fabric squares which were then pieced together on the machine. The piece was machine quilted with metallic threads.

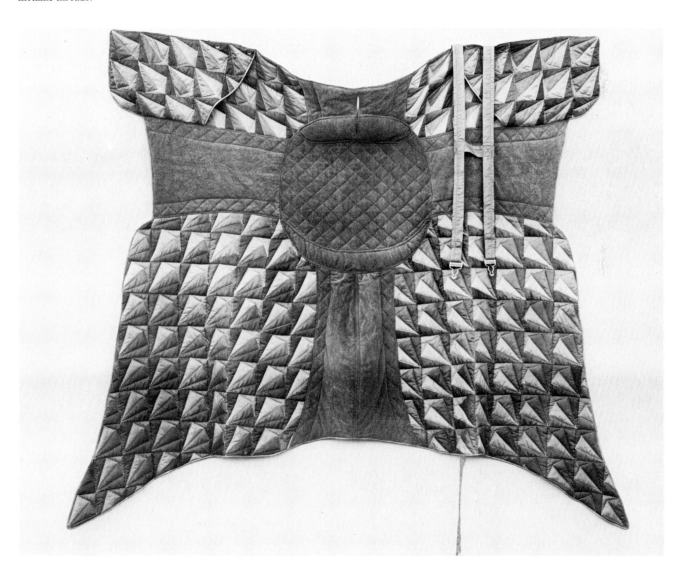

(above) *Equus Robas II*, modeled by Gladdy.

(left) *Gladdy's New Clothes*, the author. 8′ × 6′. Inspired by 16th century German suits of armor. Even though it was made to cover the body of a horse, it is considered a wall hanging. The center portion is the neck and head covering. Nylon fabric was dyed with dispersed dyes, then transfer printed and machine pieced. Metallic threads were used to machine quilt this piece.

Dress, Sandra Still. The bodice and sleeves of this cotton dress were worked with Seminole piecing.

Chapter Five

QUILTING AND TRAPUNTO

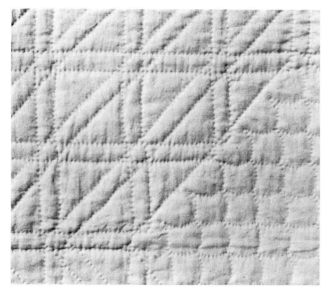

(above) **Detail of quilt on opposite page.**

(opposite) **The quilting pattern combines both curves and lines while complementing the busy overall pattern of the pieced surface. Made about 1885-90, this family quilt is owned by Carolyn Finley. The quilt has never been used or washed and still retains the pencil lines marking the quilting pattern.**

The Quilt Sandwich

Once all the blocks or pieces of the quilt have been assembled into one complete top piece, the quilting process follows. The three layers of the "sandwich"—the quilt top, the batting, and the backing—are now sewn together. The type of sewing pattern worked into the quilt is extremely important as it will not only keep the batting in place, but will enrich the overall surface design. It can also have the reverse effect of ruining a potentially interesting piece of work.

Several important decisions must be made before beginning the quilting process. As there are no rules for selecting a quilting technique or pattern, carefully consider your options. First, should the quilt be quilted in an overall pattern or tied? See Tying in this chapter. Aesthetically, some quilts require an overall pattern, and others demand the tying procedure. If quilted, should it be machine or hand worked? Some people, respecting tradition, use hand quilting exclusively, but there is an alternative. Contemporary quilts may combine hand and machine quilting. It is advisable not to spend valuable work hours hand quilting an area, or the entire quilt, if machine work will look as good or even better. Experience will help you to choose the more aesthetically correct way.

Another consideration is what type of pattern to use. There are no limits. A pattern should complement the already finished quilt top. Sometimes you may want to follow the already existing pattern, the practice in

Hawaiian quilting, see chapter 3. You may wish to contrast a pieced geometric surface with a softer, curved line quilting pattern or a curved appliqué surface with a geometric quilting pattern. This combination is often found in traditional quilts. In blank areas on the quilt, you may wish to draw and stitch a whole new image, like a portrait or flower. This approach is generally more imaginative than simply following the already existing surface pattern. However, it can be inappropriate. Consider the traditional Hawaiian quilt quilted in a contrasting pattern. Unthinkable!

(left)
Notice how the quilting follows the leaf pattern just as in the Hawaiian quilting. This quilt was made by the Santa Rosa Quilt Guild in 1979 and is owned by Kathleen Allen.

(below) This old quilt is a fine example of using curves and lines in a quilt pattern to complement its appliquéd surface. The quilt is owned by Carolyn Finley.

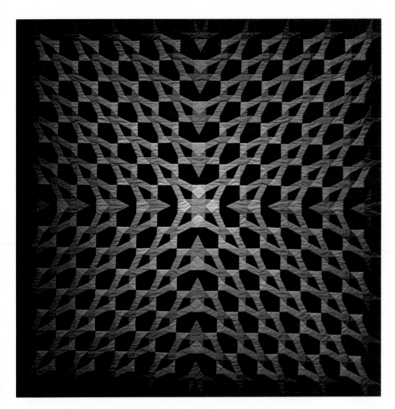

Night Flight, © Christina Buck. 110″ × 110″. Made of cotton and cotton blends, this quilt was pieced on the sewing machine and quilted by hand. Photograph by the artist.

Day Dreams, Night Dreams, Pat Rutledge. 32″ × 30″. Made of bleached cotton muslin, the surface of the quilt is created by batik. Polyester fiberfill is used as the stuffing material and has been hand quilted. Photograph by the artist.

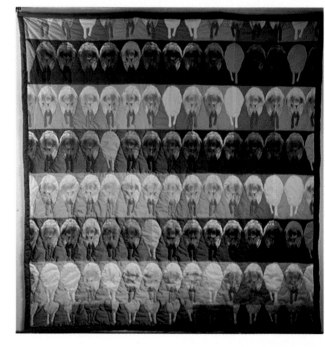

(above) *Nefertiti's Headband*, Kerry Vander Meer. 12″ × 9″ × 9″. This piece is made using gold threads on cotton, nylon, and silk fabrics. It is made by batiking, stuffing, hand appliqué, and embroidery. Photograph by Gary David.

(top, right) *Dovecote*, Marna Goldstein. The doves are made of photo-silkscreened viscose rayon taffeta. A dove pattern has been hand quilted on the satin coat. Photograph by the artist.

(right) *Ewe and The Night and The Music*, Marna Goldstein. 93″ × 90″. The cotton poplin fabric has been photo-silkscreened with fiber reactive dyes. It has been pieced and hand quilted. Photograph by the artist.

Here is another example of using curves and lines to complement the quilt surface when quilting. Courtesy of Kathleen Allen.

Besides considering the pattern itself, consider the weight and type of batting. Bonded battings will offer more freedom of design than unbonded batting. You will be able to include larger unquilted spaces in your design when using bonded batting as it will not fall apart. A thicker batting will create a deeper relief than a thin one. The depth of the relief will create a play of light and shadow on the surface of the quilt which is as important as the actual quilting pattern itself. There will also be more "take up" with a thicker batting. That is, the overall size will become smaller when quilted.

During your planning process, look at many quilts, old and new, and make several sketches. The extra time spent on preparation will help you make the best choice and will ensure more satisfaction with the result. Remember the old adage: "If it is worth doing, it is worth doing well."

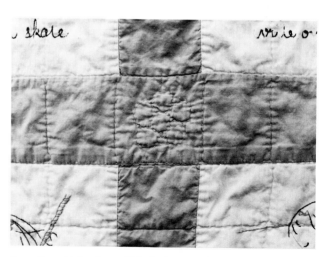

A small rosette has been stitched where two bands of contrasting cloth meet. This is a detail of a crib quilt stitched for me by my grandmother.

Predrawn quilt patterns come in various sizes. Perforated patterns or those printed on plain paper (as in the photo) are available. Other patterns come with a sheet of plastic as well as a paper design to enable you to make your own stencil. You may also buy stencil patterns already made.

Transferring Patterns

You may draw your own patterns or buy predrawn patterns for quilting. Using your own ideas may be most satisfying. However, combining purchased patterns in a creative way offers an alternative solution if you lack confidence in your own drawing. Experiment creating patterns with simple shapes. When circles, squares, rectangles and other shapes are overlapped they create new forms and ideas.

(below) The fern pattern on this old quilt is a classic. Courtesy of Kathleen Allen.

(opposite) Study the quilt surface itself to get ideas for quilt patterns, then take advantage of the piecing and appliqué work. A long thin pattern will fit nicely into a border and you may be able to fit a flower in a corner. Both of these detail photographs are from the quilt made by the Santa Rosa Quilt Guild in 1979. Courtesy of Kathleen Allen.

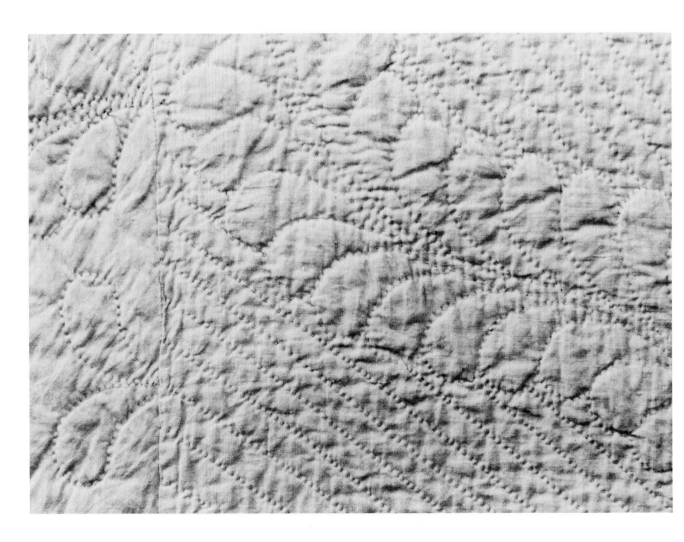

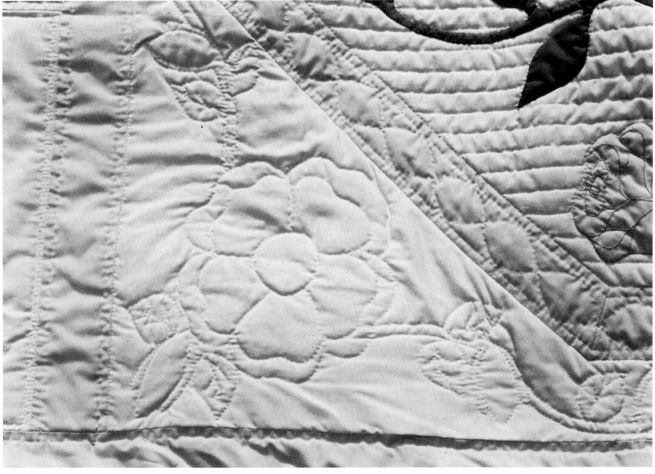

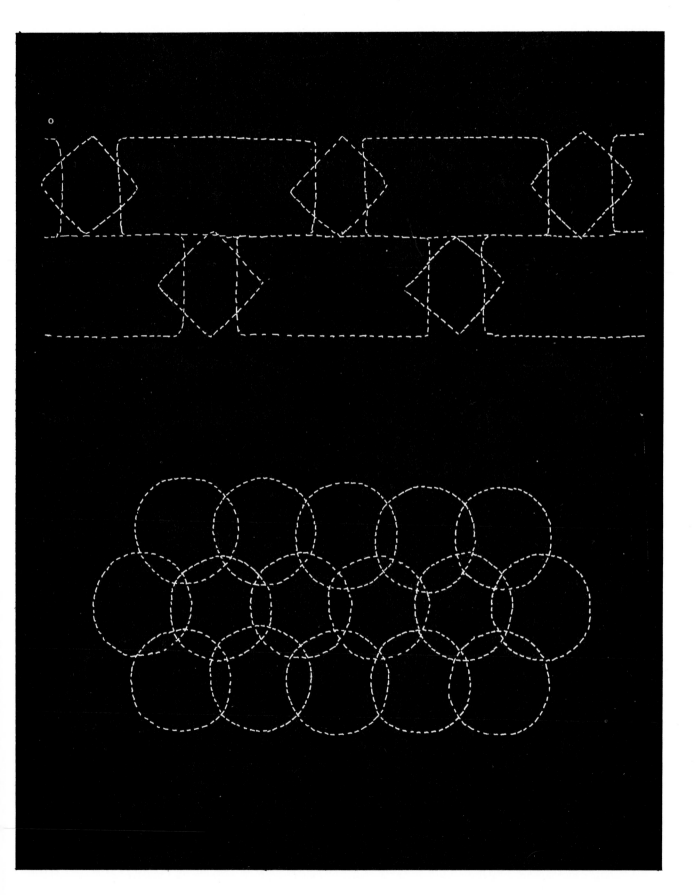

A soap sliver is being used to mark this pieced surface.

The first step is to get the quilting pattern transferred to the right side of the fabric. Again, there are no rules as to how this should be done. You must select the technique that works best for the design and fabrics you have chosen. Before you begin, it will be necessary to press your fabric very well. It is impossible to transfer a pattern onto a bumpy surface. The easiest transfer method is to draw directly on the fabric with a sharp pencil, disappearing pen, tailor chalk, or soap sliver. You may work freehand or use a yardstick, ruler, stencil, or template. A more indirect method of marking is to use a heat transfer pencil, dressmaker carbon, or transfer paper. The latter techniques are best for curved line patterns, see chapter 2.

When transferring a pattern, work with a small area at a time. As it is important to do an accurate job, rest for a while when you tire. If working with a direct method like a pencil and yardstick, carefully measure and draw lines on your fabric. If using a small unit design to be repeated several times by a stencil, transfer paper, or other means, make a few plans. As the pattern should be transferred accurately and in the proper place, use a guideline when placing your

drawing down on the fabric. If possible, use the grain of the fabric or the sewn lines of the surface to guide you. You may want to make small registration marks on your fabric in pencil before beginning. Every quilt will require its own imaginative work plan. Then, your design should be pinned or weighed down on the fabric before you begin to copy. When the copying is complete, move the design to the next area of fabric to be marked. Continue the process.

At a quilting supply store you may purchase a perforated pattern, one made by a series of small holes. It is secured to the fabric by pinning or weighting it down, and then a material like ground cinnamon is rubbed through the holes. Remove the pattern. A pencil is used to draw on the cinnamon line. Then, lift the fabric to shake off the cinnamon. This type of perforated pattern may be made at home. Simply draw a design on a heavy piece of paper (like construction paper or brown wrapping paper). Now, stitch over this line on the sewing machine (no thread, of course) using a large needle and a fairly large setting of stitches per inch.

(above) This rose pattern was first drawn on tracing paper with a heat transfer pencil. It was then transferred to the fabric by applying the iron.

(right) This arrowhead pattern is being transferred by using a stencil and by marking it with a soap sliver. The stencil was cut from light-weight cardboard and is being held in place by hand. Notice how the bottom of the stencil rests on the seam line and the side rests on a registration mark.

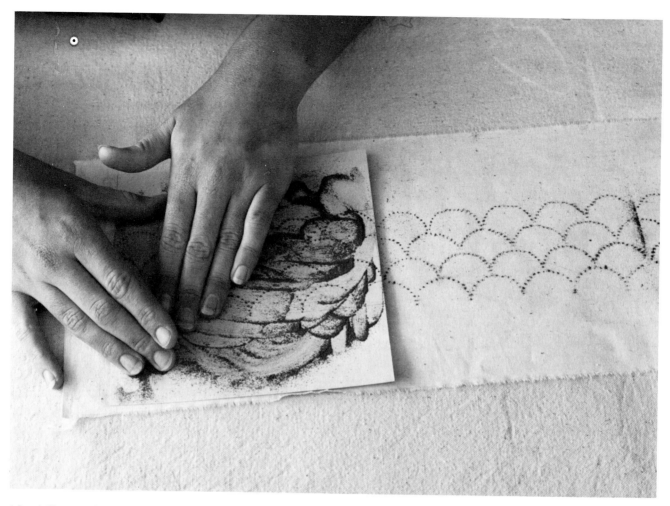

(above) Cinnamon is being rubbed through a homemade stencil.

(right) Perhaps this old quilt was marked using cinnamon and a stencil. Notice the remaining pencil lines. Courtesy of Carolyn Finley.

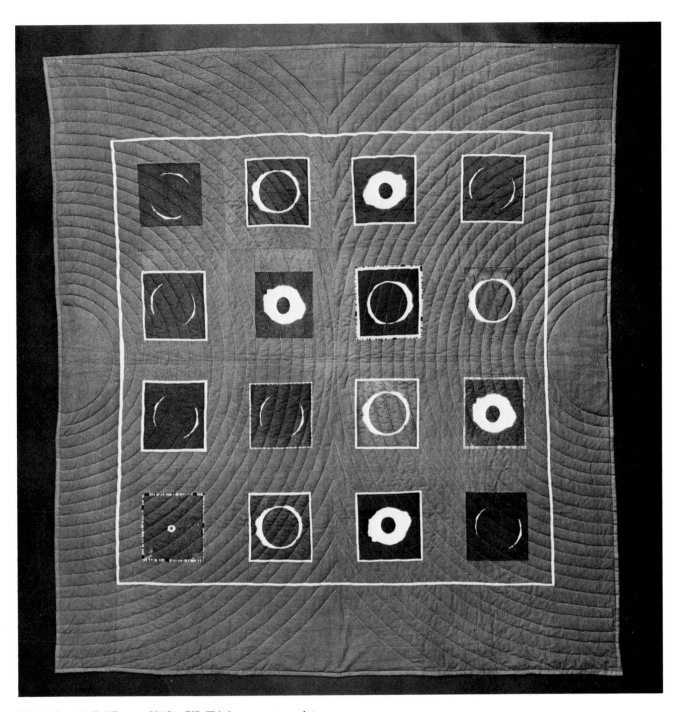

Solar Eclipse II, Tafi Brown. 80½″ × 72″. This is a cyanotype print on cotton fabric. The machine pieced, hand quilted work has polyester batting. Photograph by Michael Gordon.

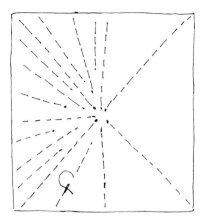

(left) If you are not following a drawn design but are following the surface pattern of the sewn pieces, simply quilt on each side of the seam line. Quilt courtesy of Carolyn Finley.

BASTE FROM THE
CENTER OUT

Preparing the Sandwich

Some quilting procedures, such as those following an already existing surface pattern, will not need any surface marking. When doing this type, omit the first step (getting the pattern on the quilt surface) and begin by pressing the quilt top and the backing very well. Now lay the backing out on a very large, flat surface with the wrong side up. Place the batting on top by rolling it out so you will not move the backing. Put the quilt top carefully on top of the batting with the right side up. Now, straighten out all three layers so they will be smooth. Starting from the center and working toward the edges, pin them together to hold in place. Now baste in the same direction.

Basting the sandwich is done very carefully to prevent any slippage and puckering that may occur while quilting. The whole process of basting begins in the center and goes toward the edge to work out any bubbles and to keep all three layers flat. Use a thread of a contrasting color. Do a good job using many lines of basting. The galloping stitch may be used to baste, see Strip Piecing in chapter 4. If you plan to use the galloping stitch and wish to machine quilt your piece, work the stitch on the back side of the quilt. If you do not, the long floats that occur on the surface undoubtedly will get caught in the sewing foot of the machine. Then do the actual quilting work while looking at the top of the quilt. How well you prepare the sandwich will determine the ease with which you quilt. Any bubbles in the quilt now will be there at completion.

After pinning the sandwich together, baste thoroughly. Always begin in the center and work out to remove any bubbles.

Quilting

Quilting may be worked using a quilting frame, a hoop, or with no support. A frame has the benefit of always being set up and available if you wish to take advantage of a few free minutes. It also allows friends to join in the quilting process as there is plenty of room for all who wish to help. A standard quilting frame is rectangular and close to the width of the quilt. You can sit at any of the four sides and work comfortably. A good height for a quilt frame is about dining table height. To attach the quilt to the frame, one end is sewn to a canvas flap on a bar of the frame. The quilt is then rolled on the bar until its other end is within easy access and can be stitched to the canvas flap on the frame's opposite side. The tension is then tightened so that stitching will be comfortable. As the quilting progresses, the finished area may be wound around the quilt bar.

Quilt hoops are very easy to use, are quite portable, and are held on your lap. They are adjusted as any embroidery hoop until the tension is just right for stitching.

Sometimes quilting may proceed without a frame or hoop for support. In this case, good preliminary basting becomes even more valuable as it is the only support. However, this technique is not advisable for a beginner. But sometimes you may not feel comfortable using a frame or hoop, or your piece may be made of materials that do not fit well into a support. For instance, if creating an art piece, parts of your quilt made of paper or of heavy upholstery fabric appliqué may not ease into a hoop. In such a case, place your quilt on a large flat surface or on your lap while stitching. You may not be able to make stitches as close together as with a frame or a hoop, but small stitches may not be vital to your project.

(above) Linnea Davis works on a child's quilt. This quilt, mounted on a quilting frame, is made from fabric pieces from the 1940s that have prints of small animals and flowers. Hearts are being stitched on the plain blocks. Photograph by Jerome Darryl.

(right) *Kaleidoscope*, 74″ × 88″. Linnea Davis uses a quilting hoop while restoring a quilt made with fabric from the 1920s to the 1940s. Photograph by Jerome Darryl.

The quilting may be done on the machine or by hand using a quilting needle and quilting thread, see Needles in chapter 2. However, you may choose to use other than the traditional quilting materials. First, select the thread. Work with whatever color or type thread will serve your purpose and complement your quilt. You may need to purchase a special needle to accommodate the thread you select.

The quilting stitch is a simple running stitch, see page 96. Traditional hand quilters will work about eight to twelve stitches per inch. But, you should do the kind of quilting that your quilt demands. If your piece is a wall quilt, and will never be used, a loosely sewn running stitch may be very appropriate to your overall piece. In this case remember the thread will be more visible and also weaker. This is also true of machine stitches. If your quilt is very traditional, stick to the more traditional quilting look. Or, perhaps you feel the quilt calls for a stitch that is ornamental as well as functional, see chapter 3.

Always use a fairly short piece of quilting thread. If you use a long thread because you do not like to thread needles, you will create problems. The thread will wear out and break if it is too long, and the quilted area will not be as strong as it should be, due to the "worn out" thread. Long thread also has a tendency to twist and knot more often than short thread. Begin a row of stitching by making a small knot at the end of the thread. Insert the needle through the top layer of fabric. The knot should be pulled through this layer and should embed itself in the batting. When you run out of thread, make a *backstitch* at the end of the quilting line and run the needle and thread under the surface fabric, through the batting, and then up about an inch from the backstitch. Clip off the thread.

Try to develop a rhythm to your stitching. It will make the process faster, more relaxing, and will help to develop straight, uniform stitches. One way to create rhythm is to use one or two thimbles while you work. You will need one on the finger that pushes the needle through the quilt and another on the finger of the other hand that "feels" the needle as it comes through the layers of fabric. If you prefer to work with bare fingers, you will prick them occasionally. Be sure to wash out any blood stains on the fabric immediately with cold water. Work your quilting stitches from the inside out, just as you did the basting. Try to work parallel lines in one direction at a time if this is possible. This procedure will help prevent bubbling. If you did a good job basting, your quilting should be an easy and relaxing job.

When hand quilting close to the edge of your quilt (and using a hoop), you will need to add strips of fabric to these edges in order to facilitate the stitching. Cut long strips of a scrap fabric. Baste them to the sides of the quilt. This will give you additional width so that when you do the hand quilting on the edge of the quilt, you will have enough fabric to fit into the hoop and keep the tension while stitching, see illustration. When the quilting is completed, remove the strips of fabric.

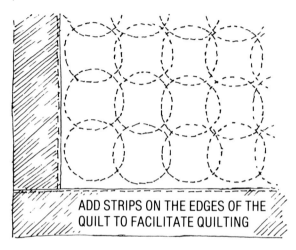

ADD STRIPS ON THE EDGES OF THE QUILT TO FACILITATE QUILTING

Machine quilting is fast, but it does have drawbacks. The home sewing machine will not easily accommodate great amounts of fabric and batting into the space to the right of the sewing foot. If you are creating a large quilt, consider making it in sections, quilting them, and then sewing them together by hand. These joinings can be made to be quite invisible, see Quilt-As-You-Go in this chapter and chapter 4. If your quilt is a comfortable size with which to work, simply fold or roll up excess fabric as you work. Make a sample first, using the actual fabrics of your quilt, to see if these fabrics create any special problems while being worked. Some fabrics, like satins, may cause puckering and slippage. Sometimes it helps if you stretch your fabric on the seam line while sewing. Hold one hand behind the sewing foot and the other hand in front. Gently stretch out the fabric as sewing proceeds. Another way to prevent puckering and fabric slippage is to use a roller foot on your machine, see chapter 2. Check with your sewing machine dealer for tips on how to sew on certain fabrics if there seems to be a problem. When you are ready to do the machine sewing on the quilt, place it under the sewing foot. Carefully flatten out the immediate sewing area so there will not be any bubbling and so you will not accidentally stitch into another area of the quilt.

Three Quilted Elements, Judy Alexander. This is an installation piece made for Fiberworks' Gallery, Berkeley, California. The strips have been made of cotton and taffeta. After the pieces were stuffed, they were tied using silver beads. Photograph by the artist.

(left) When machine quilting, it sometimes helps to stretch out the area to be quilted on the machine.

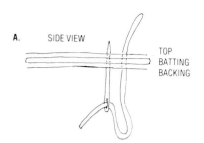

A. SIDE VIEW

TOP
BATTING
BACKING

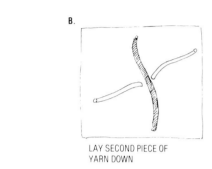

B.

LAY SECOND PIECE OF
YARN DOWN

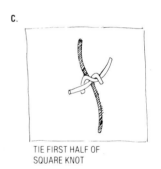

C.

TIE FIRST HALF OF
SQUARE KNOT

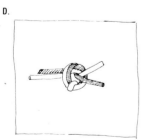

D.

TIE THE SECOND HALF
OF A SQUARE KNOT
INCLUDING SECOND
PIECE OF YARN

Tying

Quilts are often tied instead of quilted together. This technique is fast, easy, and saves time. However, many potentially nice quilts are ruined by being tied when they should have been quilted. It is very important to know whether to quilt or to tie your quilt top. Quilting not only finishes but complements and is an absolute necessity to the design of some quilt tops. But, many types of quilt tops do not benefit from quilting at all. An example of this would be any surface created in a "puff" technique, see Biscuit Puffs, this chapter. Any stitching done between the puffs to hold the front to the back will go unnoticed. Also, many surfaces of pieced quilts are so colorful and busy that quilting may be a waste of time. In this case, tying is definitely the technique to use. Whichever way you choose to complete your quilt, make sure your decision is based upon the needs of your quilt and not on how long it will take to complete.

The actual ties may be made any place that will benefit the quilt. They are often put in the corners of each square but may be used more often if desired. But remember, the number of ties, their placement, and their color will all affect the surface of the quilt. If your ties are of a contrasting color, they will show up. If you want them invisible, use a yarn that matches your surface and do the tying on a patterned fabric. Another technique is to tie the yarn in the opposite direction so it will be seen only on the back side. If a tie is placed in the center of a plain fabric, it will definitely be noticed. Thick battings and many ties will create a soft, "lumpy" looking surface. Take all these factors into consideration before beginning.

When tying a quilt, the batting must be bonded as it will not be held in place as securely as when quilted in an overall pattern. Lay out your backing, batting, and top as usual, and pin them together. Use a needle with an eye just large enough for your yarn. Thread it with a one yard length of acrylic yarn. (Other strong ribbons, cords, and threads can also be used.) From the top the needle is driven down through the three layers of cloth and out the bottom. It is then worked back up to the top. Cut the yarn off at about 2″ on each end. Now lay a second piece of yarn (about 4″) over this area. With the yarn ends that pierced the cloth, tie the first half of a square knot over the additional piece of yarn. Now, tie the second half of a square knot, including the ends of the added piece of yarn. Clip off the ends to the desired length.

Monotony, B. J. Adams. 50″ × 50″. The piece is two and one-half times the size of an actual Monopoly board. It is done in shades from gray to black, and the foundation fabric is polyester gabardine. Folding in the middle just like the real game board, it has markers and other three-dimensional pieces. Silver lamé, satin, pellon, felt, cotton, and grey sweatshirt fabrics are used. All the lettering and designs were machine embroidered. The piece was machine quilted. Photography courtesy of Pennsylvania State University.

The Pavement of Heaven, **Radka Donnell. 62″ × 88″. Radka Donnell and Claire Mielke worked together in the same way for this quilt as for** *The Long View of Love*. **Radka is a former painter who now makes quilts full time. After starting with quilts of more traditional patterns, she now uses freer structures. Photography by Tresch & Wenger, Zurich, Switzerland.**

Two prequilted blocks are being joined together.

SIDE VIEWS

A.

CLIP
BATTING
BACK
½''

TOP
BACKING

B. SEW TOPS TOGETHER
WITH ½''
SEAM
ALLOWANCE

BACKING   BACKING

BATTING

C.
FOLD UNDER & BLIND STITCH
WHIP TOGETHER   BACKING
BATTING
TOP
FOLD SEAM UNDER

Quilt-As-You-Go

Quilt-as-you-go is the process of quilting each section or block of a quilt when you finish piecing or appliquéing it. Each section is treated as if it were a large quilt, only on a much smaller scale. This approach is advantageous for two reasons. Your quilt is easier to handle because you quilt one small section at a time. And each section is portable for hand quilting and offers ease of handling if machine quilted.

Begin this technique by laying out your three layers of the quilt sandwich and pinning them together. Baste them together as you would a large quilt. You will need to save a ½" seam all around the piece in order to be able to seam one piece to another. So when you do your hand or machine quilting, do not stitch closer to the edge than ½".

When you have quilted at least two pieces, you may join them. Clip the batting away from the edges ½" all around. Now, put the tops together and sew them on one edge with a ½" seam allowance. This seam should not be opened, but folded one way or the other. This is stronger than a seam that has been opened. Open up the two pieces and lay them flat. Whipstitch the two pieces of batting together. The backing fabric must now be blindstitched in place by hand, see page 22. Fold back one edge of backing to create a ½" hem while the other edge is tucked under it.

Sew several of these quilted pieces together to create a long row of any length you wish. Then sew several rows together to create the desired width of the piece. This is the same way a "pieced quilt" top would be put together before quilting.

The biscuit puff on the right is stuffed and pinned. It is now ready to be stitched on all four sides. On the left, biscuit puffs have been put together like a "nine patch." When several of these nine patches are put together, the dark puffs forming a diagonal line will be viewed as a design element.

Biscuit Puffs

Biscuit puffs are easy, fun, and are quilted as you work. Each puff is small and portable. Scraps of fabrics may be used since each puff is only about 3" square. Two types of fabrics are needed. The top piece should be a lightweight fabric that is soft and will "puff up." The backing fabric may be a muslin or other plain fabric.

It is advisable to work with a small number of fabric squares at a time instead of trying to cut enough squares to make an entire quilt all at once. Cutting will become boring and your workmanship may grow careless. Working with nine puffs at a time, a construction similar to that of the "nine patch" block, see chapter 4, makes a good plan. Cut nine pieces of top fabric and nine pieces of backing fabric. The top pieces should be 4" square and the backing pieces 3" square. Of course, you may make this square larger or smaller according to your needs. As the dimensions get larger, the top piece of fabric also must get larger in proportion to the bottom, and the reverse is true as the dimensions get smaller.

First, with wrong sides together, lay the top piece of fabric on the bottom piece and pin them together at all four corners. The top piece of fabric will not fit perfectly onto the bottom fabric. Take a piece of stuffing and put this between the two layers. This stuffing may be any kind of material you wish. A polyester filling material used to stuff toy animals or dolls is an easy material with which to work. Now pin a tuck on each side of the square. The square now may be machine sewn all around the perimeter using a ¼" seam allowance or less. Now, sew three puffs together in a row. Create three such rows, and then sew the rows together to create a nine patch. The colors may be arranged in interesting light and dark variations which will develop when sewn together with other nine patch "puff" sections.

When the surface is completed, it may be backed with another piece of fabric. This fabric should be pinned in place. A thin layer of batting may be used between the surface and backing, but it is not necessary as the piece is already stuffed. Tying the backing to the front is the best finishing technique, see Tying this chapter.

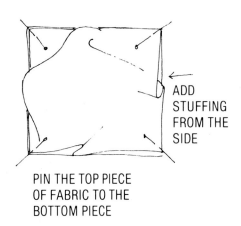

ADD STUFFING FROM THE SIDE

PIN THE TOP PIECE OF FABRIC TO THE BOTTOM PIECE

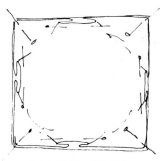

PIN A TUCK ON ALL FOUR SIDES

Sunshine and Shadow ©, Shirley Frost. 54″ × 54″. This wall hanging was inspired by the traditional Amish pattern of the same name and is an expression of Shirley's feelings about the hour before sunset.

Sunshine and Shadow ©, Detail.

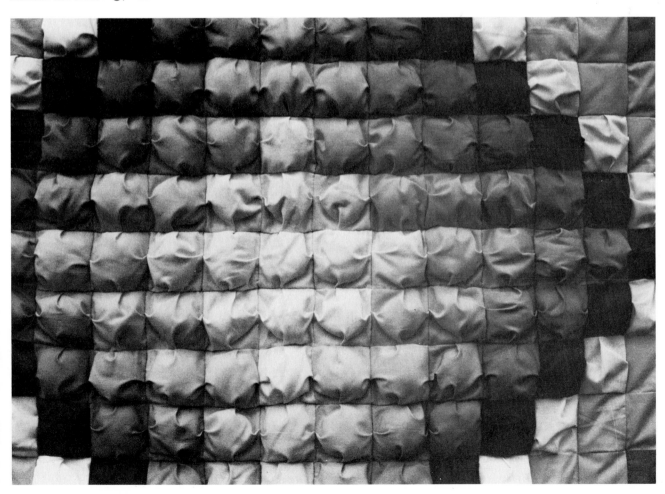

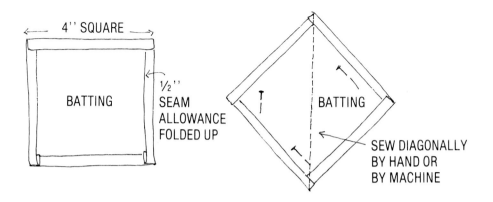

4'' SQUARE

BATTING

½'' SEAM ALLOWANCE FOLDED UP

BATTING

SEW DIAGONALLY BY HAND OR BY MACHINE

Triangular Puffs

You may make an entire quilt from small pre-quilted triangular puffs. Actually, squares and rectangular puffs also can be made, and these shapes may be combined with the triangles to create an interesting surface. Templates or direct marking are used to pre-pare the fabric for cutting.

To make a triangular puff, cut two 5″ squares of fab-ric. This will make your finished piece 4″ square since you will use ½″ seam allowances on all sides. Now cut two 4″ squares of bonded batting. You will need one square of batting for each square of fabric. Press ½″ seam allowances on all four sides of the two fabric squares. Lay the batting on the wrong side of the squares and then fold the pressed seam allow-ances up over it. Put both right sides of these two pieces together and pin. Machine or hand stitch from corner to corner. You are sewing through two layers of batting and two layers of cloth. Open to expose the right sides of the fabric. Whipstitch the edges to-gether along the pressed seam allowances. When several of these pieces have been made whipstitch them all together by hand, see page 41. Stitching by hand gives you a reversible quilt.

Squares and rectangles are easy to make also. Cut two pieces of fabric the desired size and put the right sides together. Sew them together on three sides only. Turn the piece inside out, press, and stuff with a little bit of stuffing. Close the fourth side of the square or rectangle by hand. These pieces may then be hand whipped to others to create a reversible quilt.

This triangle puff shows the seams pressed so that they fold around the batting. Notice the left side being whipstitched closed.

Trapunto

Quilting is undoubtedly the predecessor of trapunto. Trapunto, a high relief decorative design, is more dramatic than quilting because the area around the design is flat. Trapunto designs grew out of a desire to decorate the garments and furnishings of the wealthy. Originally it was worked on solid color linen fabric, but as it became more decorative it was worked on wool, cotton, silk, taffeta, and satin. Today it may be worked on printed fabrics and combined with other techniques. Since trapunto is defined by light and shadow, care must be used when combining it with a printed fabric as the trapunto work may become lost if not worked into the right piece of cloth.

Trapunto may use one or two layers of fabric. There are special requirements for these fabrics. The fabric must have the ability to be sewn easily by hand or by machine; some fabrics are simply too heavy to be used in a home sewing situation. The fabric must also have "give," the ability to stretch and ease, so that it can be molded over the stuffing or cording which creates the design. The cloth must also be compatible with the design. For example, a delicate design will not be compatible with a loosely woven cloth as the delicacy will be lost in the weave. In addition, if making clothing, be sure the fabric and material used for stuffing are compatible and prewashed.

As with other techniques, a design may be drawn freehand on the fabric or planned on paper and then transferred to the fabric. Tracing paper, transfer pencil, template, stencil, or dressmaker tracing wheel with carbon, may be used, see chapter 2. Once the design is on the top layer of fabric, the back layer may be basted in place. This back layer need not be the same cloth as the front. It may be a more loosely woven fabric, advantageous for easing the stuffing process. When the basting is complete, the permanent sewing may be done. Either machine or hand stitching may be used to sew along the drawn line.

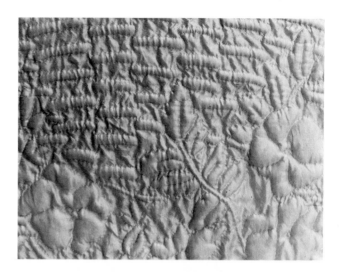

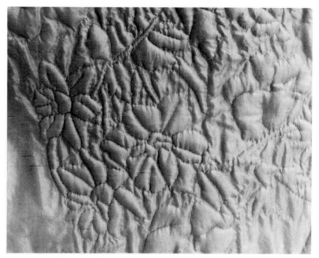

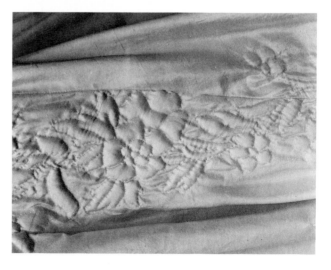

Detail photographs from a trapunto wedding dress by Ann Emlein.

Crystal Mountain, © **Jeffrey Gutcheon. 60″ × 75″. At the time this piece was created, Jeffrey was reading** *The Snow Leopard* **by Peter Mathiesson, which is about the search for the great monk of the Crystal Mountain monastery. The piece was machine pieced, hand appliquéd and hand quilted with cottons, blends, and silk. Photograph by Myron Miller.**

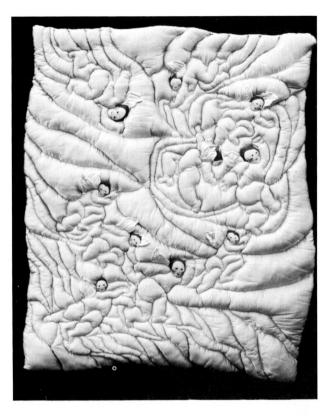

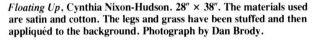

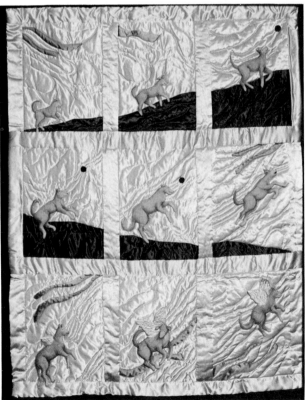

Floating Up, Cynthia Nixon-Hudson. 28″ × 38″. The materials used are satin and cotton. The legs and grass have been stuffed and then appliquéd to the background. Photograph by Dan Brody.

Ten Cherubs, Cynthia Nixon-Hudson. 62″ × 72″. This quilt was made of tinted muslin appliquéd onto satin fabric. Other techniques such as pen and ink drawing, piecing, and trapunto are employed. Photograph by Jeanne Stevens-Sollman.

Sky Rising, Cynthia Nixon-Hudson. 62″ × 76″. A pen and ink drawing on muslin was appliquéd to satin fabric. The appliqué has been stuffed. Photograph by Dan Brody.

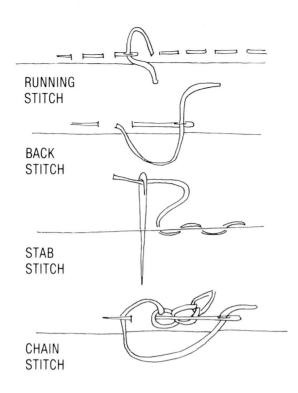

RUNNING STITCH

BACK STITCH

STAB STITCH

CHAIN STITCH

MAGNIFIED CLOTH

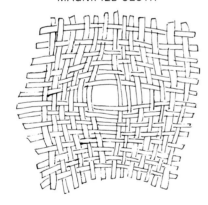

PULL THREADS OF BACK CLOTH
APART IN ORDER TO STUFF

Stuffed Trapunto

If the back layer of fabric is loosely woven, the threads may be pulled apart and bits of stuffing may be added in between the two layers of fabric using a toothpick, nutpick, or other suitable tool. When "spreading the weave," you must be careful not to poke the sharp tool through to the front layer of fabric. Carefully, pull the

threads apart using your tool while taking care not to break them. Stuff the area carefully, using the tool's point to reach into the corners. Be careful not to stuff the area too full as wrinkles and lines will form. Be careful also to pack the area evenly so it will not be "lumpy." Once the area is stuffed, close it by pulling the threads of the weave back into place.

For large areas, and when the back layer of cloth is too tightly woven to be pulled apart, the back layer may be cut with scissors. Cut according to your needs and only an area large enough for the stuffing to comfortably pass through. Be careful not to cut through the front piece. One way to prevent this error is to take a pin, prick up a few threads of backing, and lift them away from the front. Then snip the thread to create an initial hole that may be clipped to enlarge as needed. The stuffing may be cut to the exact shape of the design (if using something like bonded batting) and laid into the area. Or the area may be stuffed with bits of fiberfill. A whipstitch may be used to close the area.

Still a third technique may be employed for stuffing large areas. The top layer of fabric should have the design indicated. Then, the desired shapes of stuffing may be cut from bonded batts and laid between the top and back layers of cloth. The shapes may be first pinned and then basted in place. They then will be permanently sewn down following the edge of the batting shape. If the batting shape was cut a little too large, separate the layers of fabric and pull away the excess batting.

This shows the backing fabric of Ann Emlein's wedding dress. The design was drawn on the cotton batiste backing for the trapunto. The front or top layer of fabric is silk broadcloth. The batiste was set in place by basting after which it was permanently stitched. Then the raised areas were stuffed with acrylic rug yarn and polyester filling. Small holes were poked here and there to permit the stuffing to pass through.

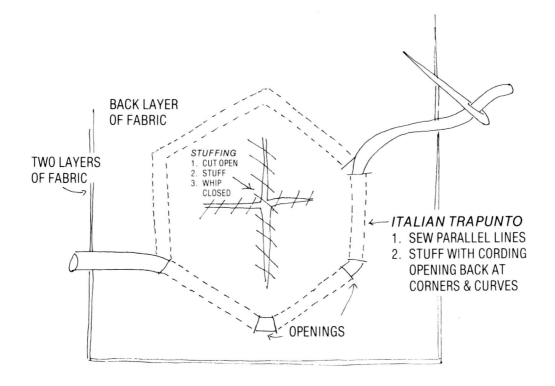

BACK LAYER
OF FABRIC

TWO LAYERS
OF FABRIC

STUFFING
1. CUT OPEN
2. STUFF
3. WHIP
   CLOSED

←*ITALIAN TRAPUNTO*
1. SEW PARALLEL LINES
2. STUFF WITH CORDING
   OPENING BACK AT
   CORNERS & CURVES

OPENINGS

Italian Trapunto

For more delicate, linear designs, Italian trapunto (also known as corded trapunto) is used. A design which consists of two parallel lines must first be drawn on the top fabric. Now, put this fabric on a backing fabric. The backing may be the same fabric as the front or a piece of soft material like thin muslin. Machine or hand sew these two pieces of fabric together on the parallel lines. The channel created may now be stuffed. Thread a blunt needle with a cord that will be compatible with your cloth. Run the needle and cord through the channel, coming up at corners and turns. A variety of cords are available for stuffing. Some are soft, while others are hard; some are single ply and others multi-ply. Some cords, like knitting yarns, are thin in diameter and others, such as ropes, are quite thick. Whichever type of cord you choose will definitely add to the character of your trapunto work.

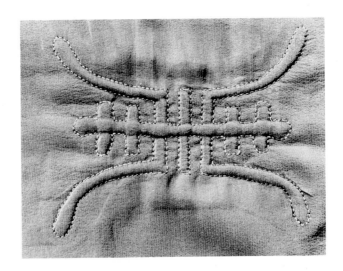

This is the logo for Fenwick of Hong Kong Limited, a clothing manufacturer. It was stitched into the lining of a tailored jacket. A very small piece of lightweight material was used as the backing fabric, and the lining was made from a lightweight crepe.

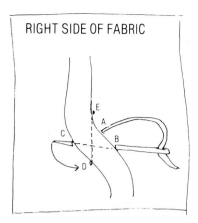

RIGHT SIDE OF FABRIC

BRING NEEDLE UP AT **A**
INSERT AT **B**
BRING NEEDLE UP AT **C**
INSERT AT **D**
ETC.....

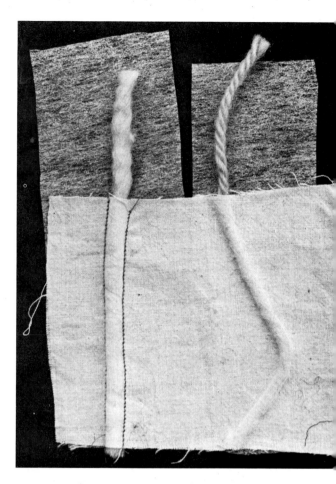

There is yet another way to create a linear design through the use of cording. With this technique, only one layer—the top layer—of fabric is used. To prepare, a single drawn line on the top of the fabric will suffice. You may also work without a plan. Whichever way you choose, practice is advised before beginning a project. A cord is laid under the fabric on the drawn line and is stitched into place. The needle and thread pass under the cord rather than through it. Looking at the top of the fabric, bring the needle up from the wrong side at point A. Going backwards, insert the needle at point B. Now, cross over and under the cord, and bring it out at C. Again go backwards and insert the needle at D. Go under the cord and bring the needle out again at E. Continue in this fashion until the design is complete.

This photograph illustrates a fast way to do trapunto. A piece of interfacing, fusable on one side only, is placed on the ironing board with the fusable side up. Then a cord or yarn is laid on the interfacing. A piece of fabric (here muslin) is then put over both. With an iron, press the areas up to the yarn but not on the yarn itself. Move the yarn around in any pattern you wish. The piece on the left has been stitched on the sewing machine with the zipper foot, after pressing. This technique probably is not appropriate for most functional textile pieces, such as clothing, but can be effective for a wall piece.

This sample shows the underside and the stitching used when doing trapunto with only a top piece of fabric.

Two Director Chair Slip Covers, **Elizabeth S. Gurrier. These delight-
ful chair covers are made of unbleached muslin, polyester batting,
and stuffing. The faces were hand embroidered. Photograph by
Hamor.**

(above) *The American Wing VIII*, Tafi Brown. 59″ × 86″. This hand quilted, machine pieced cyanotype print is done on cotton fabric. Photograph by Michael Gordon.

(right) *The Long View of Love*, Radka Donnell. 72″ × 98″. This quilt of cotton and cotton blends was laid out, then pieced by Radka on the machine. Claire Mielke did the machine quilting. Photograph by Tresch & Wenger, Zurich, Switzerland.

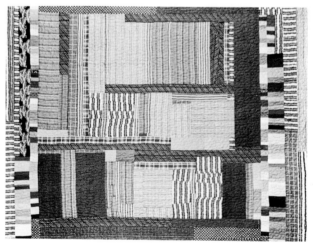

Chapter Six

NOVELTY TECHNIQUES AND FINISHES

Celtic Priests, the author. 8″ × 10″ × 12″ . This soft sculpture piece of five priests (one is hiding) is made of fabric scraps. Appliquéd patches have been made by transfer printing. The beards and hair have been done by ''mossing'' (a machine embroidery). Collection of Dr. Ruth Boyer. Photograph by the artist.

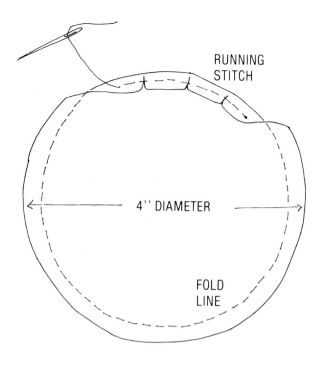

RUNNING
STITCH

4'' DIAMETER

FOLD
LINE

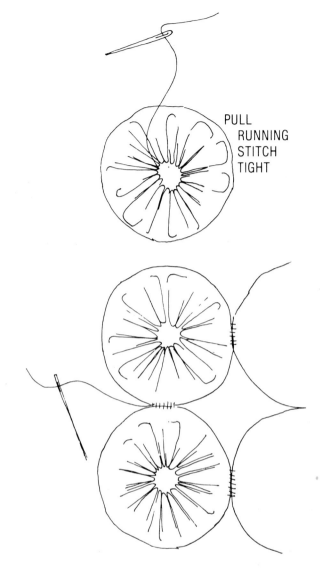

PULL
RUNNING
STITCH
TIGHT

Yo-Yo

Making "yo-yo's" is fun, easy to do, and very portable. They are made from small remnants of fabric which are put together by hand. A yo-yo quilt is not made for warmth as there is no stuffing. The surface, not a solid covering, looks rather lacy with spaces between all the individual yo-yo's. This feature and the fabric showing from underneath make it an ornamental quilt.

The first step is to cut fabric circles. A circle about 4″ in diameter is a good size. Use a drinking glass or a bowl to draw the circles on the cloth. The finished yo-yo will be about one-half the size of the cut circle.

With needle and thread, sew along the perimeter with a running stitch folding by hand a hem of about ¼″. When you have sewn around the perimeter, pull the stitching tight. This pulls the circle of fabric up so that it becomes about one-half the original size. Make sure the hem is tucked to the inside when drawing up the running thread. Secure the yo-yo with a knot at the end of the thread.

After making many yo-yo's, put them together by whipstitching the edges together for a short distance. Many rows may be made and then these rows may be joined. Continue adding yo-yo's until you reach the desired size.

This is a yo-yo sample made of cottons. Notice the pattern created by the striped fabric in the upper right hand corner.

This folded star was made with five rows. The space between the fourth and fifth rows will not show when a circular edge is cut and the piece is made into an item, like a pillow.

Folded Stars

Folded stars may be made of any size. Several smaller stars may be put together to make a large quilt or one very large star may be made and used alone.

Begin by experimenting with an average size star such as one with a finished diameter of 10". First, cut a piece of fabric 13" square. This will be the background piece on which all the folded triangles will be placed. It may be cut of the light or the dark fabric which is used for the triangles. Across the 13" square, mark diagonal lines from corner to corner.

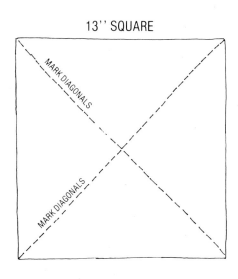

13'' SQUARE

MARK DIAGONALS

MARK DIAGONALS

You will need light and dark fabric for each star. Cut twenty-four 5″ dark squares and twelve 5″ light squares. All the squares must now be folded to make triangular shapes. First, the square is folded in half and pressed with the iron. Draw an imaginary line down the center of this half square. Fold down each corner on the folded side to the center point on the opposite side. Press with the iron.

Now, place the folded triangles on the 13″ square. Starting with the light triangles, place them in the center of the square using the diagonal lines drawn on the large square as a guide. Sew these triangles in place by hand or by machine. The second row, which is a row of dark triangles, is put down and then stitched in place. The third and fourth rows are placed, alternating light and dark triangles.

When all the triangles are in place, the edges may be cut off in a circle. Or the triangles can be continued to the edge of the fabric to form a square. The finished piece may be used alone as a pillow top or added to others to make a larger piece.

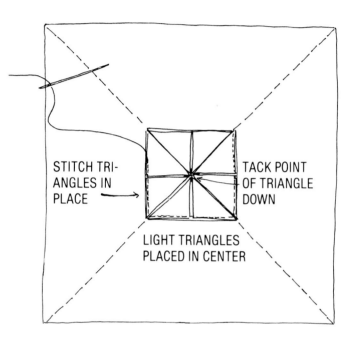

STITCH TRI-ANGLES IN PLACE →

TACK POINT OF TRIANGLE DOWN

LIGHT TRIANGLES PLACED IN CENTER

1.

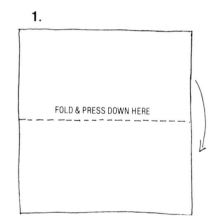

FOLD & PRESS DOWN HERE

2. FOLDED SIDE

FOLD & PRESS HERE

FOLD & PRESS DOWN HERE

IMAGINARY LINE

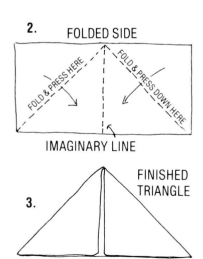

FINISHED TRIANGLE

3.

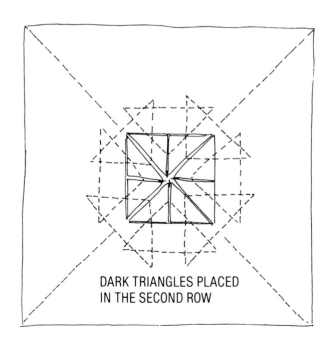

DARK TRIANGLES PLACED IN THE SECOND ROW

A Musical Box, Joan Lintault. 19″ × 17″ × 15″. Cotton fabric has been Xerox transfer printed, pieced, stuffed, and machine embroidered. The piece is a container for the working music box that sits in front. Photograph by the artist.

Cathedral Window

Making an entire quilt of the Cathedral Window pattern is a slow and painstaking process. To test your patience, try a smaller project in this interesting technique. Cathedral Windows use many layers of fabric which act as the top, the backing, and the batting. When the last square is sewn in place, the quilt is finished. The following directions will result in a 6″ square. Of course, you may change the size to accommodate your needs. Any number of squares may be joined to result in the finished size you desire. The traditional fabric to work with is unbleached muslin. Others may be used but make sure they can be creased by an iron. Avoid polyester blends for this reason.

Press the fabric well. Then, cut a template 6″ square. Cut four pieces of unbleached muslin 7″ square and four pieces of print fabric 2″ square. Lay the template on one piece of muslin so that a ½″ margin shows all the way around the edges. Press the muslin up and over the edges of the cardboard. Remove the cardboard and fold the piece of fabric in half, having the folds remain on the outside. Starting at the top on

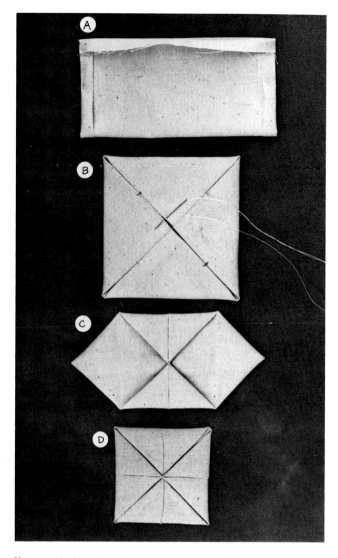

Here are the four steps for making a Cathedral Window.

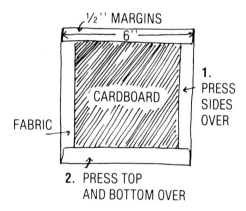

either side, whipstitch down 1½″. Now, fold the piece inside out. Ease it into place so that the large X formed meets in the center. Press flat. One line of the X is sewn and the other is not. Mark 1½″ on either side of the center and whipstitch from mark to mark. Make sure you do not stitch in the bottom layer of fabric. This is the wrong side of the square. Turn it over. Fold all the corners to the center of the X and tack them together. Make sure you tack them through several layers of fabric. Press the fabric. Your finished piece will be 3″ square. Now, make three more squares in the same manner.

Put the right sides of two squares together and whipstitch the edges of one side together. When two pairs of squares have been attached, sew them to each other. This makes one block 6″ square. Flatten out and press well.

Lay the four 2″ squares of patterned fabric on the squares formed on the right side of the 6″ muslin square. Fold the muslin fabric over the patterned fabric about ¼″ on all four sides and pin in the center. Do this on all four squares. Allow the fabric to curve naturally to the corners by putting only one pin in each side of the square. Now, blindstitch all around the patterned fabric with an off-white thread matched to muslin.

(above) The patterned square at the bottom has been laid on the muslin square. The square on the right has been pinned back on all four sides. The top and left squares have been blindstitched in place and are complete.

WRONG SIDE OF SQUARES

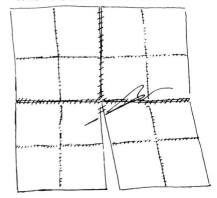

STITCH FOUR 3" SQUARES TOGETHER

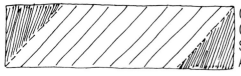

CUT OFF
SHADED
AREA

OPEN &
CUT OFF
SHADED
AREA

First, cut a piece of fabric about one-third to one-half a yard in length. Indicate the bias on one end of the fabric by folding a corner of either side over to the opposite side. A 45° angle is created and the resulting fold is the bias. Press with the iron. Open the fabric out and cut on the pressed line. Now, with pencil, indicate lines on the fabric at 2″ intervals. When you come to the end of the fabric and are no longer able to draw complete lines from one side to the other, cut the end of the fabric off just as you did at the beginning.

Now, the two long sides must be sewn together. Match up the penciled lines. Pin the edges together and sew a ¼″ seam on the sewing machine. As you will be sewing around a tube, do not try to force the fabric to lie flat while pinning and sewing together.

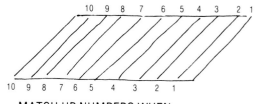

MATCH UP NUMBERS WHEN
PINNING AND SEWING

A TUBE IS CREATED
WHEN PINNED

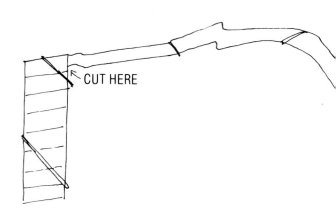

CUT HERE

Bias-Box, Bias-Bag Plaited, **Linnea Davis. 5″ × 5″ × 6″. This piece was made with purchased bias tape which was hand printed with an eraser stamp. Tapes have been sewn together to make the fabric doubly thick. The cloth was plaited and then tacked with metallic thread. A total of 136 yards of tape went into the construction of this box/bag which can be rearranged to create a box (which is pictured) or a bag with a strap handle. Photograph by the artist.**

Bias Strips

Bias strips are used often to finish the edges of quilts and quilted garments. They may be made in different widths to match and blend with the piece itself or made to contrast.

Making Bias Strips

The *bias* is the angle directly between the warp and the weft where the fabric has the most stretch. Bias strips are easy to make and to apply. The following technique is fast and eliminates sewing several small strips together because the sewing is done in one long section.

With heavy fabrics or with any that you want to lie perfectly smooth, press open the seam. This will be done most easily on the sleeve presser of your ironing board. Now, cut the one long strip of bias tape. Start cutting at either end of the tube. Cut around the tube on the penciled line.

The next step is to press the edges of the tape inward. The easiest way is to use a bias tape folder. The tape is inserted into one end of the metal holder which will fold the sides of the tape ½" inward on each side. As the bias comes out the other end, you must press these folds flat with the iron. You will have a finished width of 1". Depending upon your purpose, you may wish to press the tape in half again. If you do not have a bias tape folder, measure and press by hand.

If you wish to make a short length of bias tape, there is no need to sew a length of fabric in a tube. Simply find the bias as you did before, and cut the fabric. Mark a line for the width of bias you need and cut. If your length of bias is not long enough, join it to another length by sewing the two strips together at right angles. Joining is done on the straight of the fabric.

Using a bias strip folder speeds up the process of pressing. It also is more accurate than folding by hand.

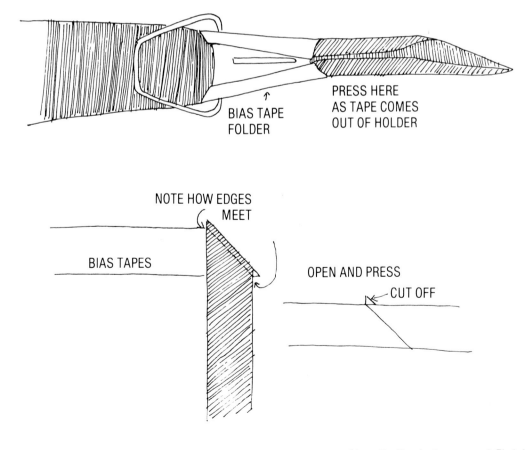

BIAS TAPE
FOLDER

PRESS HERE
AS TAPE COMES
OUT OF HOLDER

NOTE HOW EDGES
MEET

BIAS TAPES

OPEN AND PRESS
CUT OFF

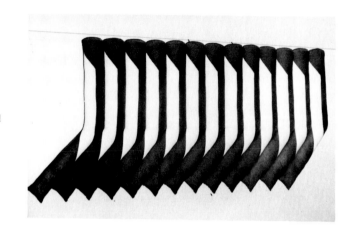

(right) *Wall Mattress IV*, Janet Levin. 42″ × 96″. The fabric has been silk screen printed with vat dye. The tubes were machine stitched and then filled with dacron polyester fiberfill. The tube ends at the top were closed with circular pieces added on by hand stitching. Those at the bottom were closed by stitching flat. Photograph by the artist.

(below) *Sour Lemon*, Janet Levin. 4″ × 3′ × 6′. The fabric was silk screen printed with vat dye. Tubes were machine stitched, stuffed with dacron polyester fiberfill, and then closed by hand stitching circular pieces on the ends. Photograph by the artist.

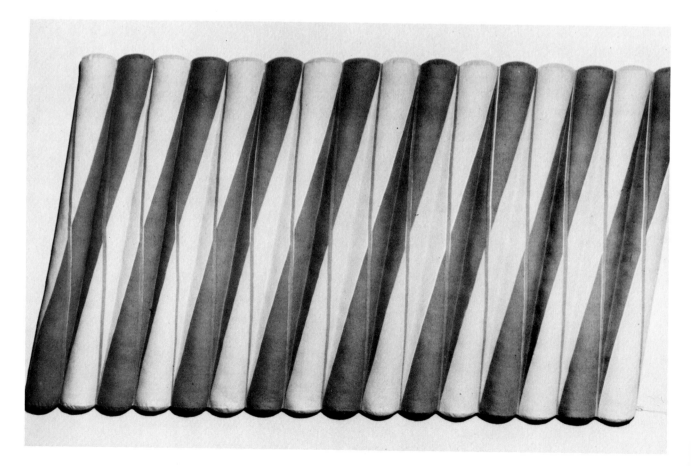

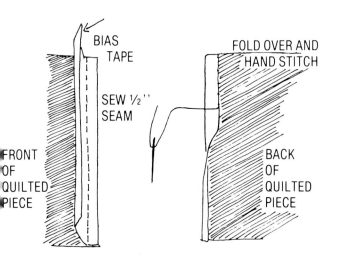

BIAS TAPE

SEW ½'' SEAM

FRONT OF QUILTED PIECE

FOLD OVER AND HAND STITCH

BACK OF QUILTED PIECE

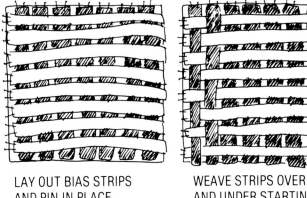

LAY OUT BIAS STRIPS AND PIN IN PLACE

WEAVE STRIPS OVER AND UNDER STARTING AT THE LEFT SIDE

Applying Bias Strips

Here are two techniques for applying bias strips. You may know others or be able to develop ones yourself.

Looking at the top of your quilted piece, pin the right side of the folded and pressed bias strip to the edge of the right side of the quilt. Machine stitch along the ½" seam allowance. Then press the bias strip outward. Fold over to the back of the quilt and stitch the ½" fold under by hand with a blindstitch, see Blindstitch in chapter 3.

Another way to finish with a bias strip is to double the tape. The tape becomes stronger and is ideal for cloth that receives a lot of wear. Instead of pressing the edges of a 2" bias tape inward on each side, press the piece of tape down the center only. Apply the raw edge side of the tape to the edge of the right side of your quilt. Stitch on the machine with a ¼" seam. Then press it outward. Bring it around to the back and stitch it by hand to the back, sewing along the fold of the tape. If your quilt is heavy or if you want a wider tape, simply cut the tape wider initially.

Weaving with Bias Strips

An interesting fabric may be created by weaving bias strips together. It can then be used in a variety of ways: to make a quilt, pocket, collar, or cuffs; or to shape a sculptural form. Any size fabric may be made. Small squares or rectangles may be woven and later sewn together. An entire quilt can be made in one woven piece using very long bias strips.

Decide on the size of your finished piece. Cut a piece of lightweight backing fabric of that size. With pins mount this fabric on a piece of cork or celetex board to hold it in place. Now, make bias strips as described in the previous section. Cut them the length and width that you need. Lay out all the strips on the fabric covered board. Pin the strips along the top and one side. Weave them together starting at the left side.

When the weaving is complete, remove the pins along the side and top. Pin the tapes together with the backing along the four sides to prevent the outside tape from sliding off. Now, sew along the edge by hand or machine to make the strips secure on the backing. The piece now may be handled as any piece of fabric. You may want to tack it to the backing fabric here and there if it is a large piece.

You may cut your bias tape fabric in other shapes. Just pin and sew around the perimeter after cutting.

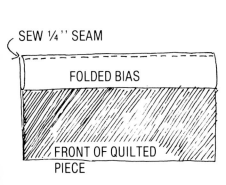

SEW ¼'' SEAM

FOLDED BIAS

FRONT OF QUILTED PIECE

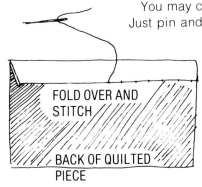

FOLD OVER AND STITCH

BACK OF QUILTED PIECE

MITERING A CORNER

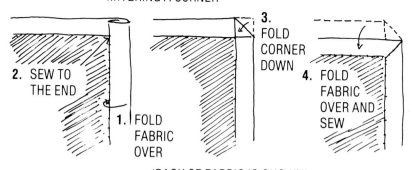

2. SEW TO THE END

1. FOLD FABRIC OVER

3. FOLD CORNER DOWN

4. FOLD FABRIC OVER AND SEW

(BACK OF FABRIC IS SHOWN)

Self-Binding

Self-binding may finish the edges of a quilted piece if you have allowed extra fabric on the top or back layer of the quilt. Bring the top layer down over the bottom or the back layer up over the top of the quilt. The amount of extra fabric needed depends upon the thickness of the batting. A very thick batting will need more fabric to allow it to reach around and then be tucked under for a small hem. Usually about 1″ extra fabric is enough.

First, decide if the top is to go over the back or the back is to come up over the top. Make sure that the edges of the backing or top and batting are cut evenly. Fold the extra front (or back) fabric over to the back (or top) and pin it in place. Before pinning down the fabric make a small hem of about ¼″. Stitch it in place with a blindstitch, see chapter 3.

A 20 Part Horse/Soldier Sloper, **the author. 17″ × 29″ × 44″. These soldiers were pieced and stitched from scraps of fabric, then sewn together. Photograph by the artist.**

Diamond Division, © Esther Parkhurst. 48″ × 48″. This quilt is 100% cotton. It was machine pieced and hand quilted. Photograph by Ken Parkhurst.

Études de Courbes, © Francoise Barnes. 75″ × 75″. This pieced quilt was constructed with cottons and cotton/polyester broadcloth and was then hand quilted. Photograph by the artist.

Vertical Quilt, Pat Hickman. 2½″ × 1½″. These hexagon pieces are
made of playing cards, gut (hog casings), and space dyed thread.
They are hand stitched. Photograph by the artist.

Pillow, the author. 12″ × 9″ × 6″. The cotton knit fabric was hand printed with a potato and then quilted with silk threads. The foundation material is foam rubber carved with an electric carving knife. Photograph by the artist.

Glossary

Appliqué A piece of fabric laid on and then stitched to the background fabric. Traditionally, it is curved rather than geometric.

Appliqué (or Embroidery) foot A foot attachment for the sewing machine used while doing machine embroidery.

Appliqué stitch A tiny hand stitch used to appliqué one piece of fabric to another.

Backstitch A strong hand-worked stitch. It goes backward and forward, forming a continuous stitch similar to a machine stitch. It may be used for sewing, embroidery, or securing the end of a stitching line.

Ball-point needle This sewing machine needle for knit fabrics prevents threads from breaking and raveling.

Ball-point pen Used to rapidly mark fabric for cutting.

Batting The stuffing material in the middle of the quilt sandwich. It creates warmth and a dark and light surface pattern.

Beeswax Threads that tend to twist while being hand sewn may be coated with beeswax. It also strengthens the thread.

Betweens Needles used for hand quilting.

Bias The 45° angle found directly between the warp and the weft where the fabric has the most stretch; a diagonal line of direction across a woven fabric.

Binding A strip of fabric sewn to the edges of a quilted piece. It finishes the edges, keeps them from raveling, and adds an element of interest, see Bias Strips and Self Binding in chapter 6.

Blindstitch A stitch used for hemming, or whenever the sewing is to be invisible.

Block The basic unit in the overall quilt surface, composed of many smaller pieces of fabric. One block is repeated many times to create the top of the quilt, see Developing Patterns in chapter 4.

Blocking The shaping of a piece of fabric. There are various ways to block fabric, weavings, and other materials. In general the fabric is pinned to a pressboard marked with the required measurements, moistened with water from a spray bottle, and then pressed lightly with a pressing cloth between the iron and the surface. When the fabric is thoroughly dry, it is removed from the board.

Borders May be added to finish and frame your quilt, just as a mat may finish a watercolor.

Calico A calico print fabric has a small floral pattern which contrasts with the background. Today it may be a plain cotton cloth or possibly a knit fabric.

Challis This printed or plain, soft, light fabric may be woven of wool, cotton, or synthetic fibers.

Chintz Chintz is a plain woven cotton fabric with a bright floral design. It has a glazed finish and is often used for drapery and upholstery.

Clipping Sometimes fabric must be clipped from a seam allowance on curves and corners. Clipping reduces bulk so cloth may be pressed to lie flat.

Comforter A comforter is a one-color quilt. It has three layers quilted together: a top, stuffing, and bottom layer.

Cross-grain The width of the fabric from selvedge to selvedge, also known as the weft.

Disappearing pens (spit pens) Excellent for marking fabric for quilting. The marks disappear when moistened.

Draftsman (plastic) triangles Come in different sizes and angles and may be used to draw directly on fabric or to make a stencil or template.

Dressmaker carbon A traditional tool used to mark fabric for sewing. It is excellent to use in preparation for cutting or quilting.

Felt markers Convenient for marking fabric for cutting.

Fiberfill A material made for stuffing toys, pillows, and other items. It is a loose, fluffy polyester material that may be purchased at the fabric store.

Fusable interfacing Interfacing that has a sticky material on one side that bonds it to another fabric when the heat of an iron is applied. Some interfacing is fusable on both sides.

Galloping stitch This basting stitch holds more securely than regular basting. It forms a Z as it works back and forth across the fabric.

Guides Sewing machine guides are used to assist you in quilting straight lines.

Heat transfer pencil Allows you to draw your image on tracing paper and transfer it to fabric by using an iron.

Hemstitch (blindstitch) Used in appliqué or hemming. The thread is hidden from view.

Hopsacking A loosely woven cloth similar to a basket weave. In this weave, two weft threads pass under two warp threads.

Leather needles Created especially to sew leather.

Lengthwise grain Sewing directions often suggest you use the "grain" of the fabric. This is the lengthwise or warp direction of fibers in a woven fabric. The lengthwise grain of the fabric is stronger than the bias or the cross-grain. If there is to be a drape on a finished piece, it will hang better if it is cut on the grain.

Muslin A plain weave cloth originally made of 100 percent cotton. Today it may be blended with synthetic materials and may be heavy or lightweight. Sometimes it is used for interfacings or clothing.

Nap The surface of a fabric. Some fabrics, like corduroy, have a raised nap. The surface appears to have two values when viewed from two different angles. A printed nap has a design. If the design is abstract, it can be viewed from any angle; if representational, such as a row of flowers with parallel stems, it can only be viewed correctly "right side up." When a fabric has no nap, it appears the same regardless of the direction it is viewed from.

Patchwork Commonly defined as fabric pieces cut and sewn together into a larger design. Actually, it relates more closely to appliqué.

Pencils Any type of graphite pencil used for marking fabric to prepare for cutting or quilting.

Piecing Small pieces of fabric sewn together to create a pattern; a patchwork is made, see chapter 4.

Piping A strip of bias fabric sewn over a cord. This finish may be used on edges or set into seams. It may be of a contrasting or matching fabric.

Preshrink Many fabrics shrink when washed. If you want to be able to wash your finished quilted piece, you must preshrink all fabrics before construction. As part of the regular fabric preparation procedure, wash fabrics according to the manufacturer's directions. It is a good idea to preshrink all washable fabric as a precaution.

Quilt In broad terms, a quilt is a "sandwich" having three layers which are stitched together.

Quilting stitch This decorative stitch holds the three layers of a quilt together. Stitches are sewn in a pattern to complement the pieced pattern.

Reverse appliqué Two or more layers of fabric laid on top of each other and tacked together. Specified areas of fabric in each layer are "cut away" to form the design.

Rickrack A flat braid, woven in a zig-zag, used ornamentally on clothing.

Roller foot A lightweight sewing machine foot good for knit fabrics and quilting.

Running stitch An in-and-out stitch. Depending upon its length, it may be used for basting, quilting, or even as a decorative stitch.

Scissors It is a good idea to have a pair of very sharp dressmaker shears, paper scissors, and thread snips. Use dressmaker shears for fabric only and never on paper as this will dull them quickly. Thread snips cut thread more quickly than scissors.

Selvedge The finished edges of the length of fabric, selvedges are more strongly woven than the fabric. It is a good idea to remove them before cutting as they may cause puckering if left on.

Set The arrangement of all individual blocks into the total quilt composition.

Sharps Sharps are the type of needle used for piecing and doing applique.

Soap sliver Good for drawing on fabric to prepare for cutting or quilting.

Stencil If a design must be repeated several times, a stencil may be appropriate. A simple drawing is made, transferred to a piece of cardboard, and cut out. The outside part is the stencil.

Tailor chalk Very good for drawing on fabric to prepare for cutting or quilting.

Template A guide for marking fabric for cutting. It may be cut from cardboard and drawn around repeatedly.

Topstitch A decorative machine stitch, sewn along an edge or seam, often in a contrasting color.

Tracing paper Thin, transparent paper used to duplicate a design. This tracing can then be transferred to a piece of fabric by "sandwiching" a piece of transfer or dressmaker carbon paper between it and the fabric. The design is copied simply by drawing on the lines.

Transfer paper Thin paper used to transfer a design from paper to fabric.

Trapunto A technique which gives a sculpted, relief effect to a piece. It is worked into one or two layers of fabric by outlining the design with stitches and stuffing it from the underside.

T square An indispensable instrument used for finding right angles. Notion companies make a wide plastic ruler that is 15″ long and 4″ wide. It is wide enough to work as a square and is transparent so that the guesswork is taken out of marking. Seam allowances may be marked with this ruler.

Tying Some quilts may be tied instead of quilted. Tying is used when no quilting pattern is needed.

Warp Threads that run lengthwise on a fabric. The warp is the strongest direction of the fabric.

Weft Threads that run crosswise on a fabric. It is not as strong as the warp.

Whipstitch A fast hand stitch used to hold two pieces of fabric together. The needle and thread reach from one piece of fabric to another.

Wrinkle-free Surface treatment given to a fabric to prevent wrinkling.

Zipper foot A sewing machine attachment that can be a handy tool for making quilt finishes.

Bibliography

The Butterick Fabric Handbook. New York: Butterick Publishing, 1975.

Greider Bradkin, Cheryl. *The Seminole Patchwork Book*. California: Self Published, 1978.

Gutcheon, Beth. *The Perfect Patchwork Primer*. New York: Penguin Books, 1974.

Holstein, Jonathan. *The Pieced Quilt, An American Design Tradition*. New York: Galahad Books, 1973.

Ickis, Marguerite. *The Standard Book of Quilt Making and Collecting*. New York: Dover Publications, Inc., 1959.

James, Michael. *The Quiltmaker's Handbook*. New Jersey: Prentice-Hall, 1978.

Johannah, Barbara. *Quick Quilting, Make a Quilt This Weekend*. New York: Drake Publishers, 1976.

Johannah, Barbara. *The Quick Quilting Handbook*. California: Pride of the Forest Press, 1979.

Kapp, Capt. Kit S. *Mola Art*. Ohio: K. S. Kapp Publications, 1972.

Lewis, Alfred Allan. *The Mountain Artisans Quilting Book*. New York: Macmillan Publishing Co., 1973.

Marein, Shirley. *Stitchery, Needlepoint, Appliqué and Patchwork*. New York: Penguin Books, 1976.

Morgan, Mary and Mosteller, Dee. *Trapunto and Other Forms of Raised Quilting*. New York: Charles Scribner's Sons, 1977.

Newman, Thelma. *Quilting, Patchwork, Appliqué, Trapunto*. New York: Crown Publishers, 1974.

Stafford, Carleton L. and Bishop, Robert. *America's Quilts and Coverlets*. New York: Weathervane Books, 1974.

Seminole Patchwork. GHN 732. Good Housekeeping. New York: Hearst Publishers, 1966.

Webster, Marie D. *Quilts: Their Story and How to Make Them*. New York: Tudor Publishing, 1948.

Wooster, Ann-Sargent. *Quiltmaking*. New York: Galahad Books, 1972.

Recommended for Patterns:
Aunt Martha's Pamphlets. Aunt Martha's Studio, Inc. North Kansas City, Mo.

McKim, Ruby. *101 Patchwork Patterns*. New York: Dover Publications, 1962.

Quilter's Newsletter/Magazine. Leman Publications, Inc., 6700 W. 44th Ave., Wheatridge, Colorado.

Index